HEALING WITH ACUPRESSURE

Healing
with Acupressure

HELEN SAUL

Keats Publishing
Chicago New York San Francisco Lisbon London Madrid Mexico City
Milan New Delhi San Juan Seoul Singapore Sydney Toronto

Library of Congress Cataloging-in-Publication Data

Saul, Helen.
    Healing with acupressure / Helen Saul.
        p.   cm. — (Healing Wisdom)
    Includes bibliographical references.
    ISBN 0-658-01239-8 (alk. paper)
    1. Acupressure.   I. Title.   II. Series.

    RM723.A27 S284   2002
    615.8'22—dc21   2001047705

Keats Publishing

A Division of The McGraw·Hill Companies

1 2 3 4 5 6 7 8 9 0   DOC/DOC   0 9 8 7 6 5 4 3 2 1

ISBN 0-658-01239-8

This book was set in Bembo by Laurie Young
Printed and bound by R. R. Donnelley—Crawfordsville

Cover and interior design by Laurie Young
Cover illustration © Shelagh Armstrong

McGraw-Hill books are available at special quantity discounts to use as premiums and sales promotions, or for use in corporate training programs. For more information, please write to the Director of Special Sales, Professional Publishing, McGraw-Hill, Two Penn Plaza, New York, NY 10121-2298. Or contact your local bookstore.

This book is printed on acid-free paper.

CONTENTS

Contents

vi

Contents

PART IV
ACUPRESSURE FOR SPECIFIC CONDITIONS

ACKNOWLEDGMENTS

Many people unknowingly contributed to this book. All have been my teachers at one time or another over the last thirty-five years, and many have been major contributors to the development of body work in all of its various forms, or of acupressure.

Hildegard Elsberg went to India in the 1950s and brought back the breathing techniques of the yoga masters; she, along with Charlotte Selver, were pioneers in bringing sensory awareness and breath work to America. Both were my teachers and contributed enormously to my learning and understanding of my own body.

Dr. Isabel Biddle, D.O., and Dr. Muriel Chapman, D.O., kept traditional osteopathy alive when it was almost a lost art. Both taught me that subtle touch can heal.

Dr. Jonathon Shore, M.D., D.H.T., homeopathic physician and friend, was the first person to use acupuncture on me—and it worked!

Dr. Richard Mauss, M.D., and Dr. Brugh Joy, M.D., gave up traditional Western medicine to train so many, myself included, in the art of developing inner healing energy through meditation, and the use of inner vision to diagnose and treat. They did this at a time when "objective" and "scientific" methods dominated the medical world in the United States.

Michael Reed Gach, Ph.D., founded the Acupressure Institute in Berkeley, California, and Alice Hiatt, R.N., remains a core faculty member. Both are great students of Traditional Chinese Medicine and how it can bring healing through touch. They have contributed immeasurably to the professionalization of acupressure in the West.

I am particularly indebted to Alice, a psychiatric nurse, who became my friend and gave so generously of her time and knowledge, helping to guide me into the world of hands-on body therapy from the world of psychotherapy.

A special acknowledgement goes to Dorothea Romankiw, the now retired founder/director of St. George Homes in Berkeley. She was a great pioneer in the nonmedical treatment of profound and chronic schizophrenia. She firmly believed that a holistic approach must be used at all times. To this end, she brought to St. George some of the most talented and experienced alternative therapists from around the world. I served as the senior psychotherapist during these years. Thus began my professional journey into the world of body energy, body work, and eventually Traditional Chinese Medicine and acupressure.

Thanks go to Chokorda Gede Rae and Dr. Wyan Weda, my two teachers in Bali, Indonesia, steeped in traditional Balinese healing, each of whom has been enormously generous in giving me their time and knowledge.

And last, but certainly not least, thanks to my longtime friend, Frena Gray-Davidson, who believed in what I was doing when I first said I could write a book on acupressure, and who served as a great guide through the labyrinth of making a book happen. She has demonstrated repeatedly in her own books that writing is both an art and hard work.

INTRODUCTION

Many people in North America have heard of acupressure, but few actually practice it. Often, it will be taught in a single course or two within the context of a larger training program in general massage or holistic body work, leading to certification as a massage practitioner or therapist. Because of this approach to training, few body and massage therapists have studied acupressure in depth, though many of them use some of the points of acupressure in their practice. The fundamental obstacle they have to a deeper, fuller understanding is that acupressure is essentially a branch of Traditional Chinese Medicine (TCM) and is thus very different from what we know as massage.

Anyone can practice acupressure. You can use it on yourself and on others. As a self-help technique, it has been proved extremely effective for a variety of bodily discomforts and conditions. Used on others, acupressure can relieve pain; stop excessive bleeding; relieve the congestion of the common cold; alleviate the symptoms of arthritis, backache, slipped disk, and sprains; and abate the throbbing of a headache. Sore muscles and general tension can be relieved quickly and safely. Acupressure points have been used by women for centuries to improve their complexion and to become more beautiful. And acupressure can be used simply to promote better health in general.

There are two main reasons why fewer people practice acupressure. The first is that acupressure is rarely taught in the West. The second is that it requires an understanding of the basis of TCM, which may explain why it is not often taught in the West. For those interested in going beyond the simple introductory courses given with massage accreditation, the study of acupressure is preceded by a complex theoretical introduction of Chinese medical theory. Those who want to truly understand acupressure are often intimidated because the body of knowledge may seem far too vast and difficult to grasp. Fortunately, this is not the case.

This aim of this book is to further your understanding of the principles of acupressure—not through an extensive study of the related theories, but through a hands-on approach to its application.

There are relatively few books about acupressure in English. A few have been translated from Chinese (sometimes poorly) or from Japanese. Those in English are generally written by American or British authors who have taken a body of knowledge from TCM, as practiced in Japan, Korea, China, and other places in Asia and formulated it into the separate discipline we know as acupressure. They are they ones who introduced the term to the West. The practice of this new-to-the-West discipline has been channeled into various schools of acupressure, each with its own master teacher and followers. Various styles—ranging from very traditional Chinese massage or Japanese shiatsu to entirely new forms not seen in China—have emerged. The few books on acupressure reflect these variations in tradition and style. Most acupressurists (or acupressure therapists, as they are sometimes called) rely heavily on acupuncture books for their understanding of the function of the meridians and the meridian points central to the practice of acupressure.

Because of the very close relationship between acupuncture and acupressure, the few books on acupressure are often overly complicated and filled with Chinese terms, names, and theories. Others are so simplistic and provide no understanding or theoretical basis for the practice. These may consist merely of instructions to press such and such a point for this or that condition.

In this book, we'll attempt to walk you down a middle path. While a certain amount of terminology and theory is necessary to begin to comprehend the world of Chinese medical thought and practice, we'll emphasize learning through practice. The primary approach will be on hands-on learning, experience, and the application of a few fundamental principles.

This is the same approach used by many teachers of t'ai chi or chi gung. Some of the best instructors do not give any theory whatsoever to students until they have followed the movements daily, for weeks or even months. Eventually, once the students have found a new relationship with their own body through doing, the theory is introduced. Out of this experience the teacher can then tell the students about the movements and their significance without having to resort to intellectual explanations.

In my case, over many, many years I learned several different forms of body work, breathing practices, and structured disciplines of exercise by this hands-on method. Although I have studied the theory to a considerable extent and read a large number of books on Chinese medicine, it has been my practice on others and my experience of acupressure itself that most contributed to my understanding of it.

Theory alone does not begin to teach any single style of acupressure, nor does it offer a detailed knowledge of specifics or even provide an in-depth understanding of the underlying principles. However, using exercises as a basis for learning will provide a glimpse into the vast world of TCM. This will introduce the basics so that anyone can begin to practice acupressure, in an effective manner, even casually.

The charts will not be as detailed as those found in books on acupuncture. More detailed charts can be obtained elsewhere. By simplifying, I hope to not overwhelm the reader with what is essentially an extremely detailed and complex body of knowledge.

The annotated bibliography will serve as a guide for those who wish to pursue the study of acupressure and TCM. A list of training schools, associations, and sources of supplies and additional information is also included.

So, prepare yourself for a working study of the fascinating world of acupressure, a journey in which your hands and your sensitivities are at least as important as your mind and understanding.

PART I
THE WHOLE PERSON

1

The Traditional Chinese View of the Human Body

Acupressure, an ancient discipline, has emerged from the same misty origins as Ayurveda, acupuncture, and traditional Tibetan and Chinese medicine. The practice of acupressure in the West has its roots in this Eastern world. We cannot learn about acupressure without having some understanding of this great body of traditional knowledge. We would be learning only a technique, not a *practice* if we only familiarized ourselves with the way the Chinese view the human being and body.

This Eastern worldview, and the practice of acupressure that is a part of it, is very different from that of Western medical practices. What little is known of the beginnings of acupressure suggests that its originators had a profound awareness of the totality of the whole human being. They also possessed a knowledge of nature and the place of the human being in this larger context.

Many people in the West tend to think of TCM as an exotic practice with complex and mystical theories; some think its practitioners, doctors of Chinese medicine and acupuncture, have possible esoteric powers. This fanciful interpretation can be appealing. However, it is unlikely that many Chinese doctors would lay claim to such powers.

The Chinese are an eminently practical and pragmatic people, and their medical system is based on centuries of careful observation and documentation. This includes hundreds of volumes of medical texts written over the centuries and has resulted in one of the most complete and thoroughly researched medical systems in the world. Chinese medicine consists of a number of related disciplines, including acupuncture, an extensive pharmacopoeia of herbal medicine, and a range of sophisticated methods that we in the West would call "massage" or acupressure.

The Chinese medical system includes and stresses a recognition of the subtle life energy systems of the body. We call these energy flows *meridians,* and they were already well mapped in ancient times. One of the earliest statues known to history is a stone figure from China showing the same acupuncture points used today.

The tradition of some Chinese masters' teachings suggests that these meridians and points were originally located through mental observation alone. That is, in a meditative state, a practiced person would observe and map the subtle flows of energy within the body and its various organs. Thus, the observer could see the relationship and connections among energy flows on the surface of the body and the various internal viscera and organs.

We in the modern West may find this strange. But consider that many people have experienced or observed martial arts masters knock an opponent off his feet with energy alone, without actually physically touching the person. Most of us will never be able to achieve the degree of inner awareness that would allow us to observe the inner energy channels. Nevertheless, we can develop a new and more intimate familiarity with our bodies that will result in a vastly expanded sense of who and what we are.

It is worth repeating that while acupressure has gained wide recognition in the West today—and some forms of it have been developed by Western practitioners—we must not forget that this is not a Western form of body therapy. If we fail to understand its Chinese origins, we may never touch the true heart of the healing process.

5

EASTERN AND WESTERN APPROACHES

Usually, in Western teachings about the human body, the physiological, anatomical, and biochemical parts and processes are presented. A great deal of emphasis is on the gross anatomy and the mechanical relationships among parts. This approach has certainly led to scientific advances, but its essentially mechanistic character has also been a drawback. It has, for example, confined our vision of ourselves to the physical aspects of our existence. One consequence is that we Westerners tend to put the emotional, psychological, mental, and spiritual dimensions of our lives into areas that have little to do with our bodies. This is not so in China or other parts of Asia.

As an example that will help illustrate this radically different view of the body, consider what happens when a sick person on the island of Bali in Indonesia goes to see a traditional Balinese healer—a *balian*.

The Balian

The balian is the inheritor of a medical tradition not unlike the oldest forms of TCM and tantric yoga. The balian may or may not be part of a family lineage, but he (or, more rarely, she) is always "called" to his profession and takes up a personal regimen of both study and meditation in order to practice as a healer.

The Balinese balian generally lives in a small village and consults with clients who come to his home. The balian sees them in his outdoor consulting room, where he has the instruments of his trade: herbs, tinctures and teas, meditational objects such as tantric drawings, special diagnostic tools, a mat or couch for the client to sit or lie upon, and his *lontar* (traditional books written on palm leaf) of medical texts.

The person coming for a consultation does not come alone, as is usually the case when one visits a Western doctor. At least one family member, and usually several, will accompany the ill person. They'll enter the consulting room together, and the interactions and comments of the family are an integral part of the interview and process to understand the illness. The balian will have already done his own meditational and energy-centering exercises or will include such meditation and exercises in the process of working with his patient. The doctor of TCM and most practitioners of traditional healing arts in Korea, Japan, India, and other Asian countries also emphasize the inner state of the healer.

In addition to the use of herbs, which most balian use extensively, he will apply deep-pressure massage of key points on the body, for the purpose of both diagnosis and treatment. The balian will also make a series of hand passes—sometimes over his

6

own body, sometimes over the body of the patient—to both change the energy of the patient and, as important, to transfer "power," or energy, from himself to the patient. The balian does not see this as his power, but rather, the power of the greater universe—of nature itself. The patient sees it this way too. The balian is a "holy" man. In Bali, healing will sometimes include Balinese Hindu temple ritual. And, even if not actually using ritual and prayer with a particular patient, he is seen as connected to the greater powers of the universe by virtue of his training and calling to be a balian. The patient and family never pay the balian directly. Instead, they leave an offering, put together in the same manner as a temple offering, on the table where the balian has some of his special objects.

7

The West

The traditional medicine practiced by the balian today is probably rooted in Chinese medicine. The similarity of Balinese medicine—by including the energy meridians, energy centers, and herbology, and various practices that appear very similar to traditional Tibetan practice—points to the existence of an older tradition underlying all of these, including TCM.

The example of the balian is intended to illustrate in some detail the profound differences in mind-set or worldview between East and West, a difference that, once again, should inform us when it comes to the world of acupressure. The core view in this approach is that the human being is a part of the whole of nature. This is not a theoretical view but a part of everyone's everyday experience. It helps that in Bali the climate and fertility of the land have led to a primarily outdoor lifestyle. A person is continuously a part of and influenced by all of the seen and unseen aspects of the universe. In this world a person's daily life contains many rituals that acknowledge and honor this richness and abundance. The use of natural elements in the healing process (for example, herbs) and the reliance on energy development, exchange, and transfer to bring about the necessary rebalance, are based on the fundamental connection to nature.

Today in the West we have come to a point where we recognize that the *wholeness* of a person is profoundly important. Our popular culture is placing a new emphasis on caring for ourselves, which includes caring for our bodies. This is caring not just in the medical sense, but in a growing appreciation of our bodies as contributors to our sense of well-being, pleasure, and the richness of life.

At the beginning of the twenty-first century, we have come far from the lifestyle and attitudes of our Victorian forebears. A hundred years ago, even talking about the body and bodily functions in normal conversations raised anxiety levels and produced vague, or not so vague, feelings of guilt or shame. Over the last century, we have a generally accepted the importance of physical fitness and exercise. This has led to an enormous number of memberships in health and fitness clubs and to widespread participation in a variety of sports. We have also come to appreciate various types of massage and body therapies, forms of Chinese exercise, and different practices of Asian martial arts.

Unfortunately, this new acceptance of our bodies as part of our well-being has also taken extreme forms. Some have resorted to unnecessary plastic surgery, dangerous breast implants, the taking of deadly steroids to bulk muscle mass, and radical diets and extreme sporting activity. Clearly, we are struggling with our

Western view and experience of the human body, and we are still in the process of developing a healthy relationship with it.

Let's hope that learning about acupressure will enhance and lead to a more positive experience of your own body as you apply these techniques of therapeutic touch. As you work with the exercises, allow yourself to be led to a more integrated and whole experience of yourself and others. Perhaps you will begin to see and experience the body as part of a larger world, a world that contains more dimension and richness than you have experienced before.

9

2

The Energy of Our Bodies

Our bodies are living, ever moving and changing, creating and being recreated from the moment of birth to the time of death. We know this intuitively as well as from observation. If we pay attention, we can feel our hearts beating rhythmically. We can notice our breathing, but take it for granted and do not think about it. Nor do we think about the fact that the dynamic systems and changes within our bodies are the marvelous result of an ever-flowing movement of energy.

As discussed in the previous chapter, Western science has taken a different approach to the body than what has developed in the East, as with TCM. This is one reason why we think about our bodies as somehow separate from other aspects of who we are. In the West, we want to look at and understand systems and subsystems, parts and particles, neurons and molecules. In TCM (and Japanese, Ayurvedic, Balinese, and so forth) there has long been a reliance on body/mind energy-balancing techniques and medicinal herbs.

Western science has been able to identify some of the bio-chemical and bioelectric systems that operate as a living web, holding together the molecules and cells of our bodies. However, we know very little about other levels, such as the mind or con-sciousness. Although many in the West are aware that emotional states are directly related to and have an influence on body states, minimal attention has been paid to this fact in the field of medi-cine. Most medical treatments (with drug therapies for mental ill-nesses as a notable exception) do not really include the mind as a part of the overall health picture. In fact, a prevalent belief among Western medical practitioners is that the mind (or consciousness) and our emotional states are "caused" by the physical body. In contrast, in Chinese medicine, the condition of the emotional life is considered as important as all other factors in understanding the complex states of the body's health and functioning.

CHI

A central idea in the Chinese approach to understanding how our bodies work is that of chi. This Chinese word can be translated as "energy." But the Chinese have observed that there are many kinds and sources of energy, and each of these has a different name and is considered to be a different kind of chi.

Some kinds of chi exist independently of the human organism or any living being Chi is found in any natural set-ting—water chi, mountain chi, and so on. In Chinese, each will have its own name, but they are all part of the universal chi.

Other forms of chi contribute specifically to the life of the human and the body.

The chi energy of the body resides, or is centered in, specific key areas. The Taoists have called the three most fundamental and important body energies (and their centers in the body) the *Three Vital Treasures.* An enormous amount of exploration of these energies has been done by Taoist scholars, and the resultant books form the foundation of practice for TCM, acupuncture, acupressure, t'ai chi, chi gung, and the traditional martial arts.

For the acupressure therapist, and Chinese medicine in general, some of the more important forms of chi are prenatal chi; protective chi; the chi of breath (sometimes called *prana* in Hindu yoga texts); the chi derived from food; the chi that circulates through the various systems of our body/mind; and the chi of heart or spirit, called *shen.*

The prenatal chi is the life energy we are born with that sustains us through our life. In some people, this is very strong; in others it is weak. This concept is somewhat similar to the Western idea of "constitution." The prenatal chi can often be seen at the root of a lifelong tendency toward a certain type of illness, such as a weakness that leads to asthma or to a susceptibility to skin allergies. These predispositions have also been recognized by Western medicine, especially by homeopathy.

The protective chi surrounds the body to ward off potentially damaging influences from the environment such as cold, wind, damp, dryness, and heat. This protective energy can become depleted through stress or overexertion. A person may then become ill. Protective chi can be built up with specific exercise, proper diet, breath, and physical arts such as chi gung.

13

The food we eat and the air we breathe are constant and ongoing sources of energy for our bodies. Westerners are aware of this and may try to pay attention to it. However, a great deal more attention is paid in TCM. For example, foods are regularly selected for their capacity to contribute specific kinds of energy to the body. Breathing exercises are done by literally millions of people everyday to promote well-being and bring balance to the body/mind.

The worldwide practice of chi gung—a combination of breath, movement, and meditation techniques—is used to build up various forms of chi.

The body centers' primary, sustaining vital energy is a point known as *dan tien* in Chinese and as the hara in Japanese. The *hara* is located in the solar plexus, slightly below the navel. This is an important area for developing and centering energy in the various martial arts. Merce Cunningham, the famous American dancer, taught the students in his master classes to center in and move from the hara. The result was a very fluid and natural dance movement. The energy in the hara can be deliberately nourished with breath exercises and meditation (see the hara breathing exercise in Chapter 5), although the original source of this energy is the prenatal chi.

The energy of the shen, or spirit, is the transformed energy of life chi. It is centered in the heart and is a central part of the goal of enlightenment. The shen is energy built upon strong body chi, right living, the practices of spiritual development, and living out unconditional love. It is overlooked by many Western practitioners of yoga, t'ai chi, and the martial arts. Its importance in Chinese Taoist tradition is obvious in that it is one of the Three Vital Treasures.

MERIDIANS

In the West, the best-known description of chi is the flow of energy in the body that circulates through the meridians. The flow of chi in the meridians is the primary focus of acupressure and acupuncture.

From a Chinese point of view, meridian flows are most important to the health and well-being of the body. Each meridian is related to a system of functions and organs such as the heart, lungs, and stomach, and each contributes to the balance and coordination of these various systems within the body.

One translation of the Chinese word for the meridian-energy system of the body is "a silken network of pathways," or the Silken Pathways, implying qualities such as soft, subtle, strong, and invisible. TCM identifies twelve main meridians, each related to the various organs of the body, as well as many subsidiary and connecting channels. These channels run on both the body's surface and internally. Identifying the imbalances of energy flow that develop in the body through these channels and rebalancing them are at the heart of all of the traditional Chinese healing arts, including acupressure.

All of the meridians are actually meridian complexes, and each is related in various ways, forming a great network of functioning and weaving a pattern that touches every area of the body.

The meridians are very much like rivers and streams. Essential energy flows through and nourishes the areas of the body to which they are near. Large and small, each meridian is a path of circulation and influence coursing through the organs and between each other, forming a connecting web that supports, vitalizes, and regulates the entire body and all of its functions.

15

It may appear as if the meridians are subdividing and partitioning the body, but in fact the meridian complex is one great whole of flowing energy, changing quality and intensity as it moves throughout the body.

The Chinese describe fifty-nine energy channels, divided into five categories:

1. The twelve main meridians, which are associated with the organs of the body and which we usually see in acupuncture charts as the focus of treatment
2. The fifteen connecting meridians *(luo)*
3. The twelve muscle meridians, which run on the surface of the body and are almost identical in path to the main meridians
4. The twelve divergent meridians
5. The eight strange flows, or so-called "extra meridians." These have received attention recently in the West in certain forms of acupressure such as Jin Shin or Jin Shin Do. These are the only meridians that share points with the main meridians.

Each of the meridians has changing and fluctuating amounts of essential energy, ebbing and flowing with the time of day, the seasons, and the state of the person. And, as with rivers and streams, these channels can become blocked or stagnant, or flooded and excessive in their action and force. In acupressure, just as in acupuncture, we work with this flow of energy in the meridian channels in order to restore balance and harmony.

You will never have to learn all of the channels. They are listed to give you a larger picture of the sophistication of the

Chinese understanding of the body. Most acupressurists never learn more than the pathways and points on the main meridians and the functions of the "strange flows," or extra meridians. This book will give you an overall picture of the location of the main meridians and some of the most useful points. And, more important, you will learn how to feel for and recognize meridians and points without the use of charts and without having to memorize locations.

YIN AND YANG CHI

All of the meridians are divided into two categories, according to the overall general quality of the chi energy: yin or yang. The idea of yin and yang is central to Chinese medicine. They are seen as inseparable forms of energy, each dependent upon the other. Lao Zi wrote:

> *The tao gives rise to one.*
> *One gives rise to two.*
> *Two gives rise to three.*
> *And three gives rise to the ten thousand beings.*
> *The ten thousand beings all carry yin on their shoulders*
> *And embrace yang in their arms.*

Yin is generally described as feminine and of the earth, water, winter, harvest, and dark. Yang has masculine qualities of the sky, fire, summer, and light. These are not opposites; rather, they are imagistic terms used to describe fluctuating cycles of change and complimentary states of being. So, in the great symbol of the yin and yang, the dark area has a spot of light within it, and the light part of the symbol, a spot of dark.

The idea of the coexistence of yin and yang in everything is central to Chinese medicine. The balance of the two maintains health, and imbalance leads to illness.

Each of the organs and functions associated with the meridians is known to have a predominantly yin or yang quality as shown in Table 2.1. For example, the lung meridian and the actual lungs are said to be yin. This makes sense when you think of the nurturing functions of the lungs in drawing in "the breath of life," a form of chi that the Chinese say combines with the chi from the food we eat in order to sustain bodily life.

TABLE 2.1	THE YIN AND YANG ORGANS
The main yin organ meridians	Lung, spleen, pericardium, liver, heart, kidney
The main yang organ meridians	Large intestine, stomach, triple warmer, gall bladder, small intestine, bladder

Note: Even though the organ meridians are referred to as being either yin or yang, we must remember that each is related to the other, and the quality of the one is always contained in the other.

The chi of the main yang meridians flows *down* the body, and the yang meridians are generally located on the harder, less protected areas of the body. The chi of the main yin meridians flows *up* the body, and the yin meridians are generally located on the softer, more protected areas of the body.

To best visualize this flow of chi, one can look at the body as a bridge linking heaven and earth in a standing, upright position, the arms and hands upstretched toward the sky, feet on the earth. In this position, the main yin meridians channel chi from the feet on the earth, up the legs, into the torso, and up the arms to the fingertips pointing to the sky. Conversely, the main yang meridians channel chi from the hands in the sky and down into the torso, through the legs, and into the feet on the earth.

While many books in English describe the yin meridian as running "down" the arm to the fingertips, this is merely a description of a chart on which the arms are at the side of the body. It is not an accurate explanation of the direction of energy flow in a yin meridian. The yin energy does not move down—it moves up the body. Likewise, yang meridians do not channel energy up the arm, even though the chart position of the arms may lead one to say so. If the basic image of the body extending between earth and sky is held in mind, you will avoid confusion about the direction of energy flow in the main meridians.

In working on the body, we want to enhance the natural flow of energy in the meridian. Ultimately, this natural flow is all we are working with in acupressure. By learning the basic direction of this flow, you will always be in a position to feel and direct it with your hands, so it's important not to be confused by the charts.

FIVE ELEMENT THEORY

At some point during the development of Chinese medicine, the Taoist view of nature developed another understanding of the way chi flowed through the meridians and what the relationship between the various meridians was. In Chinese medicine this is called wu xing, translated into English as the Five Element Theory.

Ted Kaptchuk, in *The Web That Has No Weaver,* points out that *wu* translates to "five band," and *xing* implies movement and change, and therefore a more accurate translation is Five Phase Theory. This is not a theory about "things," or fundamental elements of matter. This is a way of describing the movement and change of energy in cycles or phases and the changes in the body reflecting the changes observed in nature.

The Five Element Theory, almost three thousand years old, developed independently of the yin and yang way of defining things. There are many books on acupuncture and acupressure that never refer to the Five Element Theory. When it is present, it is often used as a theoretical schema to explain the *results* of treatment. It is not, in general, a part of the *diagnostic* method or *process* of treatment, as is the yin/yang approach.

The five phases of energy are:

1. Wood
2. Fire
3. Earth
4. Metal
5. Water

These are related to the seasons of spring, summer, Indian summer, autumn, and winter, in that order. Each phase describes a function:

- Wood is a growing phase.
- Fire designates maximum activity leading to change.

- Metal describes a declining phase.
- Water is a phase of inactivity and rest about to change direction.
- Earth is a place of balance.

Each phase is related to a pair of organs and meridians in the body.

In general, the Five Element Theory has been both misunderstood and misused in the West, but in the practice of acupressure, it is not necessary to understand it in detail. I've gone into it because it is so often found in other books. Perhaps the most useful part of the Five Element Theory is to remind us that we are, indeed, part of the larger world of nature and all of its seasons and cycles. This idea can become lost in our modern industrial society, and we suffer because of it.

The practice of acupressure, as has already been noted, is fundamentally based on these concepts. It is very hard to read about acupressure without some familiarity with them. However, in your practice you may use only a few of these. They have been presented here to help illustrate and expand the conceptual framework within which acupressure exists. Perhaps it will help guide you as you explore and develop your knowledge of acupressure.

21

3

Traditional Methods of Enhancing Life Energy

Acupressure is an integral part of Chinese medicine. In the West, it is generally practiced outside of the medical world. While acupressurists are neither treating illness nor practicing medicine, it is important to understand why acupressure is a part of Chinese medicine and why it can be used outside of its medical applications.

Chinese medicine is fundamentally a system of observing and balancing the energy systems of the body to restore and maintain health, even in the face of negative factors. Because of this, acupressure is eminently suited for maintaining and promoting health and well-being outside of a medical practice.

The energy of the human body is subtly flowing, much like the channels, eddies, and bayous of a great river. The delicate web and pattern of this energy flow can become stagnated or flooded, or weak or excessively strong, producing imbalances and illnesses.

Chinese medicine provides us with ways of looking at these imbalances.

CAUSES OF IMBALANCE

Imbalance is brought about in three main ways:

1. Through the influence of external events and conditions, the so-called *external evils*
2. Through changes in the internal condition of the person, primarily due to changes in the *five primary emotions*
3. Through the invasion of severe *pathogens*

External Evils

The external evils recognized by the Chinese are wind, cold, summer heat, dampness, dryness, and fire. These are seen as reflective of the six kinds of seasonal climates. Extremes and rapid changes can be overwhelming to the body's capacity to adjust, and they lead to an abnormality in the person's yin and yang balance. Thus, certain illnesses are seen as closely related to the seasons. Chinese medicine has extensively observed and documented the subtle effects of the external evils on all of the body systems and the wide range of dysfunctions that can result.

Five Primary Emotions

The internal factors that can result in disharmony are the primary emotions, which are connected to each of the major internal organs:

1. Joy
2. Anger
3. Anxiety or Pensiveness
4. Grief or Anguish
5. Fear

Each of these emotions is fundamental to human life. If they are excessive, bottled up and unexpressed, or overwhelmingly activated by circumstance, they can create stresses that lead to severe imbalance and illness.

Table 3.1 illustrates how each of the primary emotions is related to one of the organ meridians of the body.

TABLE 3.1	RELATIONSHIPS BETWEEN PRIMARY EMOTIONS AND THE MERIDIANS
EMOTION	MERIDIAN
Joy	Heart, small intestine
Anger	Liver, gall bladder
Anxiety or pensiveness	Spleen, stomach
Grief or anguish	Lung, large intestine
Fear	Kidney, bladder

While Westerners may see some of these emotions as negative or positive, from the Chinese point of view they are basic to human nature and therefore in need of balance and structure. The causes of diseases that are brought on by emotional stimuli

25

reside completely within the organism, and Chinese medicine has many approaches to rebalancing the system related to these factors.

Pathogens

The pathogenic factors include contaminated food, poisons, environmental toxins, and epidemics of pathogenic micro-organisms (viruses, bacteria, parasites, and so forth). However, a person's susceptibility to these pathogens is seen as related to his or her internal state.

DISCIPLINES WITHIN CHINESE MEDICINE

Traditional Chinese therapy has developed many ways to influence these imbalances. When external influences—environment, trauma—or the internal influences of a person's habits—emotions, lifestyle—have resulted in illness, changes can be deliberately made to return the flows to a proper balance within their channels. A properly trained practitioner can influence the body's energy flows to bring about predictable changes with a high degree of accuracy and beneficial effect.

The techniques used to change the body-energy flows in Chinese therapeutic practice are broadly grouped into several (overlapping) disciplines:

- Acupuncture
- Acupressure
- Moxabustion and cupping

- Physical exercises
- Meditation
- Herbology

While none of these methods excludes the other, they are dealt with separately because in practice, they are often done by different practitioners or by practitioners who place a greater emphasis on one over the other. An acupuncturist will include the use of moxabustion and cupping as well as the use of herbs but won't necessarily prescribe meditation or physical exercise disciplines. On the other hand, a practitioner of one of the schools of physical exercise may often use acupressure as well as meditation.

Acupuncture

In acupuncture, the trained practitioner (in China, Japan, or Korea it's generally a doctor of traditional medicine) inserts needles into specific points on the energy meridians. These needles generally are very fine and sharp, and usually there is little, if any, pain during placement. The needles are inserted to the required depth and left for varying lengths of time, from a few minutes to a half hour or so, sometimes being turned or vibrated to stimulate the points.

27

An acupuncturist will choose the points based upon a careful evaluation of the quality of flow in the various meridians. The diagnostic techniques to make this evaluation include measuring the pulses in the wrists for each of the meridians; observation of the person's color, demeanor, tongue, and so forth; and an interview. The acupuncturist will use needles only after a diagnosis has been made. Acupuncture is most often used to treat severe illness (usually in conjunction with herbs) and for chronic illness.

Acupuncture is not a self-help technique and should not be practiced by an untrained person. This cannot be stressed strongly enough. Besides the obvious issue of needing sterile needles, remember that when they are inserted into the body, there is always a danger of puncturing a vein or artery. Using acupuncture needles safely takes a great deal of specialized training, including a detailed knowledge of anatomy. Also, needling is very powerful and can result in sudden and extreme changes in the body. For example, the use of needles can produce an anesthetic response strong enough to allow painless surgery.

Moxabustion and Cupping

In moxabustion, the meridian points are stimulated with heat that comes from burning an herb called *moxa,* a variety of artemisia (in the West we also call it mugwort). With its fuzzy, soft leaf, moxa is used both in a rolled form and as a loose herb.

Moxabustion is generally carried out so that the burning herb never touches the skin. (In some traditions in China the burning moxa was allowed to touch the skin and scarring occurred. This scarring became a sign of valor among some men.) Keeping the moxa from burning the skin is achieved in a variety of ways. A small, tightly rolled cone of moxa can be placed on a selected point on the skin and removed before the skin is burned. Or, the skin might be protected with a slice of gingerroot under the burning moxa. A common method is to tightly roll moxa in a paper tube and burn the end of this roll. The roll resembles a cigar, and the hot tip is brought near the energy point to stimulate it by means of heat.

Moxabustion is safe to use as a self-help technique and is widely used by the general populace in Japan and China, especially in cold and damp areas. I'll discuss the specific techniques and useful ways to carry out moxabustion in Chapter 14.

In cupping, the points are stimulated by creating a vacuum over the point. The air inside a special glass cup (usually using burning moxa) is heated and then the upside-down cup is placed over the point. As the air cools, it forms a partial vacuum. This technique should not be used except by a trained person, because the vacuum formed can be quite strong, often enough to rupture the tiny blood vessels on the surface of the skin. Having a sterile environment is crucial, as well as a clear knowledge of the location and use of the points.

Physical Exercise

T'ai chi and chi gung are the two most common forms of physical exercise used to regulate the body energy and harmonize its flow. The various martial arts also have this regulating and harmonizing effect, often using techniques from chi gung, but they are not as widely practiced.

The practice of chi gung is required of all practitioners of acupuncture and is a central part of their training. This is true in North America as well as in China. The various traditional movements, and especially the breathing techniques, are understood to effect the meridians in various ways, enhance the development of internal body chi, and regulate its flow in the body. Chi gung is commonly practiced on a daily basis by Chinese people for its health-enhancing ability.

The different forms of chi gung focus on the type of breathing and its regulation, the inner control of energy flow, and the development of inner chi.

29

In this book, you will have the opportunity to learn the Eight Essential Exercises of chi gung. These exercises are ancient. Illustrations, which are more than two thousand years old, have recently been found painted on the walls of the Number Three Tomb excavations from the Han Dynasty.

T'ai chi is another form of movement exercise combined with breathing. Again, there are various forms and schools of t'ai chi, and they are included in the training of the acupuncturist and acupressurist.

In the West, some forms of physical exercise have been called acu yoga. Michael Reed Gach, author of *The Bum Back Book* and the founder and director of the Acupressure Institute of America, has used the term in several of his books. These exercises are derived from chi gung and yoga and are known to have beneficial effects on the meridian flows as well as on the gross anatomy of the body.

Meditation

In all of the above practices, to one degree or another, meditation is used to develop inner power and control, and to enhance the regulation of chi. The meditational part of chi gung is very important and is related to what has been called the "introspective view of the inside scene." In the fourteenth century, Li Shizen introduced this term in his work *A Study of the Eight Extra Channels.* He wrote, "The tunnel to the inside scene can only be observed through the reverberator." The other translation is "introspectively."

Li Shizen was discussing the much older practice of the chi gung masters and meditators who have achieved enough mental cultivation to see introspectively, observe and recognize the inside scene of the body organs, and experience the channels of the meridians.

Introspectively viewing the inside scene of the body was used to diagnose and to learn the various flows and interconnections of the energy channels. We have already pointed out that this introspective ability is the likely origin of the knowledge of the meridian flows.

There are reports that even in modern China there are those who can see the inner channels and feel the flow of chi. It is probable that many who practice meditation and chi gung can develop this ability to some degree or another. Because it's now possible to objectively locate the meridian points using modern instruments of detection, we must assume that there is an objective basis to this reported ability. It is quite likely that with correct practice, many people can develop this skill to some degree or another.

One of the main sources for the transmission of the Chinese healing arts was the Taoist temple known as *kuan,* usually translated into English as "monastery" or "temple." However, literally translated, kuan means "inner looking place" or 'inner observatory." This reveals a great deal about what the central focus of the practitioner of the healing arts must be.

Herbs

The Chinese use medicinal herbs at least as extensively as they use acupuncture. It should be added that the medicinal use of food is also universal. Medicinal herbs are used not only as they would be in the West—where a specific herb is known to have a specific effect, such as licorice soothing a sore throat—but to rebalance the yin and yang chi in the meridians when disharmony has caused illness.

The practice of Chinese herbalism is based on an extensive pharmacopoeia and is quite complex. Westerners would be well-advised to use Chinese herbs only in their patent medicine form, from known common formulas, or when obtained as a formula from a trained practioner. Many of these herbs, while readily available, are very powerful, and in a few cases, when used in the wrong way, they are potentially dangerous.

Acupressure

In the West, acupressure has been referred to as "acupuncture without needles," and also by a variety of names given to different schools of acupressure. Acupressure has many forms in China and Japan. Each form has been developed to manipulate the chi in the energy meridians by the hands and fingers, not through the use of needles or herbs. The use of hands and fingers is very specific, and a wide variety of techniques have been carefully developed over the centuries. One of the more widely known forms in the United States is that of *Jin Shin Do,* a term coined by Iona Marsaa Teeguarden. Jin Shin Jitsu is a form of Jin Shin Do taught to black belt jujitsu students by some teachers. Certain forms are known by such names as *Tui Na, pointing therapy, Amma,* and *shiatsu.* These forms sometimes look like Western massage, but they're different because they are always based upon Chinese medical theory of chi and meridians.

According to tradition, the earliest Taoist masters practiced a form of acupressure that used neither needles nor direct touch with the hands or fingers. This most powerful form of healing was accomplished simply by pointing and by the transfer of energy through conscious intention. Today, many books written by Chinese practitioners hint that this is still practiced by some masters.

Historically, many practitioners of these disciplines were blind people given a skill they could perform well and thus earn a living. Among the schools of martial arts, the practice of acupressure resulted from knowing the disabling or "death" points and also from needing the ability to heal the injured.

In the West, the forms of acupressure taught by the different schools and practiced by Western practitioners vary widely. They can range from the subtle, almost "psychic" touch of the Jin Shin Do school of Iona Teeguarden, to the extreme pressure placed on the body in shiatsu. There is Touch for Health, reflexology, the work of Bonnie Pruden, and reiki, an acupressure-like form of healing currently popular in the West. While some of these schools lay claim to Asian roots, they would probably not be recognized by TCM. On the other hand, cranial-sacral work, derived from osteopathy, is quite similar to some traditional acupressure.

Acupressure Versus Western Massage

To some, it may seem as if acupressure is like Western massage, but the ways in which the body is understood and is touched are very different. In general, in Western massage the focus has always been on the mechanics of the body and the function of the muscles. Improved circulation, the tension of musculature, and the flexibility of ligaments and tendons are the central focus. In practice, the work is done primarily on the muscles. The movement of the hands along the extremities is always toward the heart, which is seen as the center of the body, and the flow of the blood is given great importance.

In acupressure, in contrast, the focus is always on the subtle energy balance in the functions of the body. The movement of the hands on the extremities is in relation to the flow of the chi in the meridians, and the balanced functioning of the various parts of the chi energy flow and the body systems is of prime importance. The condition of the musculature, if of concern, is always secondary to the flow of energy in the meridians.

Acupressure is sometimes used in conjunction with acupuncture, especially to relax the body and open the flow of the meridian channels. It is also practiced as a separate medical discipline. Its efficacy is recognized in China and Japan, and it is used extensively in hospitals and clinics. However, acupressure can be practiced in a nonmedical setting, with nonmedical intent, just as massage is practiced in the West.

In later chapters, you will learn the elements of acupressure that are fundamental to its practice. However, the focus will be on its nonmedical applications. This is not to say that the acupressure you will learn here has nothing to do with health and healing. Acupressure has everything to do with health and healing because it is always aimed at restoring and enhancing health and maintaining balance in the total energy system of the body.

PART II

EXPERIENCING OUR PHYSICAL BEINGS

4

Sensing Our Bodies

This chapter contains exercises that will help you become more aware of your body. It is not enough to just do them once or twice; you should do them often. You are attempting to reform your awareness and experience, not just gain new ideas or thoughts.

In time, you may be motivated to turn your practice into a *practice,* a discipline of meditation and exercise done repeatedly in order to achieve mastery. This is the best way to not only shift your awareness of your body, but also to gain the inner experience that will make acupressure more than just a technique.

The next chapter will focus specifically on body energy. For now, becoming aware of our own bodies, their areas of tension or pain, and the "feel" of the various parts will help you begin to build the foundation for effectively doing acupressure.

Knowing your body's experience of tension, relaxation, how the body holds tension, and how to relax will serve as the best guide to working on someone else. This awareness of your own body is an absolute essential if you are to use self-help acupressure to help yourself and others.

Awareness of ourselves in our bodies and *as* a body requires a radical shift in our usual way of doing things. Too often, we find ourselves rushing from one activity to another, worried about time, and not taking a moment to just sit and relax without doing something else. We find ourselves suffering from a generalized feeling of tension, and specific areas of our body are often tense or even in pain. The back, shoulder, and neck areas are prone to this tension, as if we were literally carrying the burden of life on our upper bodies.

38

In fact, we have many metaphors for the general way in which we experience modern life. We "carry too much weight on our backs." Our boss is "a pain in the neck." We "can't stomach our job," our business associate, or the way we're treated by someone. These metaphors are often accurate descriptions of our physical maladies: hemorrhoids, constipation, hernias, ulcers, acid indigestion, lower back pain, shoulder pain, stiff neck—all of which are stress ailments resulting from lifestyle. Slowing down enough to experience ourselves in our bodies requires that we take some time.

SENSORY AWARENESS EXERCISES

The experiments and following exercises have been traditionally used for body relaxation and what has come to be called sensory awareness. Most of these exercises have their root origins in Indian yoga, but they were developed in the West in new ways. They have been widely taught and written about by such practitioners as Charlotte Selver, Bernard Gunther, Grof Von Durkheim, and several others trained at such places as the Esalen Institute in Big Sur, California.

These exercises are not generally taught in training programs for acupressure or TCM, yet they can be practiced prior to learning the more specific methods of breathing, such as hara breathing, which we'll discuss in the next chapter. In fact, attempting to learn hara breathing without being aware of our bodies and correcting our bad breathing habits will often lead to incorrect breathing, with the result that you will not gain the benefits it promises. Most of us have lost much awareness of our own bodies, in addition to developing poor breathing habits. Recontacting our own bodies in the ways developed by the practioners of sensory awareness can be enormously helpful.

At this point, you may be tempted to move ahead to the chapters on acupressure itself. Do not succumb to impatience. It is one of our greatest enemies and will do immense harm in the actual practice of acupressure. Instead, go slowly through this chapter, taking the time to experiment with these exercises.

Do them more than once.

Relax with them.

Learn about yourself with them.

And most of all, have fun with them. Enjoy them.

Exercise 1: Assess Your Breathing

1. In a comfortably warm place, place a folded quilt or blanket or a yoga mat on the floor to firmly cushion your body. Lie on your back. If you find that this is uncomfortable or painful in your lower back, place a pillow, bolster, or cushion under your knees so that they are raised 4 to 6 inches from the floor.

2. Close your eyes and place your hands on the floor to your sides.

3. Relax your jaw with your mouth slightly open and your tongue lying relaxed on the bottom of your mouth with the tip against your teeth. (This is different from the position used in prana yoga and hara breathing.)

4. Notice if you are breathing through your mouth only. If so, see if you can inhale through your nose and exhale through your mouth.

5. Do not do anything except focus your attention on your breathing. Do not attempt to manipulate your breathing in any way beyond what has just been described. Try to stay focused on it. Stay as relaxed as possible while being aware of your breathing. If your mind drifts to something else, simply come back to awareness of breathing and don't worry about why you drifted. Everyone does at first.

6. Now notice if you are breathing primarily with your chest expanding and your shoulders rising,

your belly expanding, in between, or all of these.
See if you can feel your back muscles expanding
and relaxing as you breathe.

Do this exercise for 5 minutes. ✂

Notes: You may fall asleep if you do this exercise when you
are very tired. No matter, try it again when you are rested. If you
have a partner, try this exercise while he or she watches and quietly reminds you from time to time to breathe and to relax. Do
this exercise at least once a week, if not daily, until you feel comfortable and relaxed with even, regular breathing.

41

Exercise 2: Belly Breathing

After you have done Exercise 1 several times,
expand it as follows:

1. After the first 2 to 3 minutes, place one hand
   over your navel and notice whether it is rising
   and sinking as you breathe. If not, focus on
   relaxing your abdominal muscles so you are
   adding what is called *belly breathing*. Do *not*
   tense your muscles or attempt to force yourself
   to breathe in any way. If you relax your abdominal muscles, gravity will work for you.

2. If your chest is not moving up and down, place
   your hand on the center of your chest. Use the
   natural pressure of your hand to focus on this

continued on next page

area and try to relax your chest so it moves with your breathing. Take a deep breath, taking in as much air as possible by expanding your chest, and then relax. Take deep breaths up to 3 times but not more. See if this helps relax your chest.

3. If your shoulders move up and down as you breathe, focus your attention on relaxing the muscles in your shoulder and neck area. Focus on breathing down rather than up. If this does not help relax your shoulders and eliminate the upward movement, do the following:

- Pull your shoulders toward your ears with as much power as you can. *Do not* tense your jaw and face while doing this.
- Hold this position only for 3 to 5 seconds and then relax your shoulders.
- Now push your right arm along the floor toward your feet as far as you can. Hold this for 3 to 5 seconds and then relax.
- Repeat with your left arm.
- Do the shoulder shrug again.
- Repeat the entire sequence up to 5 times.

4. Notice where your breathing is. Keep breathing gently and quietly and simply keep your attention focused. You should be able to feel your back against the floor and feel it expand as you breathe in. Focus for a while on this, and imagine your breath entering your body and leaving through your back into the earth.

Do this exercise at least once a week if not daily.

Note: This exercise is an enlargement of Exercise 1. It is designed to expand your breathing in such a way that it can become the foundation for both your well-being and all other breathing practices you will learn. These, together, form a strong foundation for working with body energy and doing acupressure.

Be careful not to strain in doing any part of this exercise. If you find yourself straining, stop any movement you may be doing, put your hands to your sides, and simply breathe, focusing your attention on your breathing until it again becomes slow, even, and relaxed.

By the time you have practiced these exercises for several weeks, your breathing should be more easy, full, and relaxed. Many report that they became aware of their breathing through-out their day and easily relax their breathing and entire bodies when they notice tension or if they're under stress.

43

Exercise 3: An Inventory of the Body

In this exercise, you are going to mentally scan your entire body. You are going to use your awareness to notice all of the parts of your body, and you will begin to learn how to relax your muscles.

1. Assume the position on the floor as in the previous exercises with your eyes closed.

2. Spend time focusing on your breathing until it is slow, relaxed, and rhythmic.

3. Focus your awareness on your toes. Allow your toes to relax. See if you can be aware of just

continued on next page

how each joint in each toe feels. When your toes have relaxed, shift your awareness to the main part of your feet. See if you can relax the arches of your feet. Then shift your attention to your ankles. Try to be aware of all of the muscles that surround your ankles and feel them relax.

4. Move your attention to your legs. Slowly move your awareness up the muscles in your legs, letting them relax as much as possible. Notice how your knees feel and if you can relax them more.

5. When your knees feel relaxed, allow your attention to move up your legs until you are aware of your buttocks and lower abdominal muscles. By focusing your attention to this area, moving through each small area within the pelvis and hips, you will begin to sense the different muscles and feel their state of tension. Allow each to relax. Feel your buttocks soften and your body sink more toward the earth. As your buttocks soften, you may feel the muscles in your lower back begin to loosen.

6. Allow your consciousness to slowly move up the main part of the body, while trying to be aware of each part of it. See if you can let your back open up and your chest and rib cage relax and expand. Notice if you are holding tension across your belly, and if you are, allow your stomach muscles to relax.

7. As you move up the body toward the shoulders, allow them to relax in such a way that you feel as if you no longer have to hold your head on your body or keep your arms from flying off.

8. Move your consciousness down each arm, one at a time, in the same manner as you moved up each leg. Let your elbows relax, and your wrists. See if you can feel the tension in your hands and fingers, and allow them to relax and expand.

9. Finally, become aware first of your neck and then the jaw area. Allow your jaw, cheek, and chin muscles to relax. If your jaw goes slack, allow it to do so. Notice all the little muscles around your nose and eyes and across your forehead. Let them relax. As silly as it may sound, see if you can relax your scalp.

45

Note: When this exercise is done in the context of a group or class in sensory awareness, guided by an instructor, the time allowed to complete the full body tour is generally about fifteen minutes. If your mind drifts, or you fall asleep during it, it will take considerably longer. Be certain that when you start this exercise, you allow yourself plenty of time to complete it in a relaxed and unhurried manner.

You should now be extremely relaxed and, I hope, not asleep. If you do fall asleep during this exercise, it may be a signal of stored tiredness or fatigue. Continue the exercise when you wake up, until you have completed becoming aware of your entire body.

Upon completion of this exercise for the first time, most people find they have far more awareness of their body, muscles, the body's complexity, and the areas of tension.

Review what you have experienced.

After you have done this exercise several times, your awareness of yourself will have vastly expanded. You will find that you can do an inventory of your state of body relaxation fairly quickly and in almost any position and situation. Not only will you have learned a great deal about yourself, but also about human anatomy. You will find that you can live a more relaxed life in general because you literally know how to relax.

THE REMAINING ESSENTIAL EXERCISES

Chi gung has many forms and movements within forms. The eight exercises described in this chapter are very old and have been practiced in the context of many different forms or schools. As I mentioned earlier, we know from tomb paintings that these exercises are at least two thousand years old. Yet today, they are practiced by almost everyone in China—at day care centers, in schools, and in all of the neighborhood senior centers.

They are called the Eight Silken Movements. We are reminded that the meridians are known as the Silken Pathways, and it is true that these exercises exert a profound influence on the energy meridians of the body. Each of the eight exercises stretches and strengthens one or more of the meridians. Their benefit arises from doing them daily. Because it only takes about ten minutes to complete all of them, the exercises should easily become a part of your practice.

As you progress through each of these exercises, notice what you feel, what parts of your body you experience, and what the exercises inform you about your body. This is all a part of a growing sensory awareness.

46

In doing these exercises, you must allow yourself to breathe in a relaxed manner. Later you will learn, if you do not already know, how to do hara breathing. While this form of breathing enhances the effect of the exercises, it is not necessary in order to benefit from them.

The best form of breathing is to inhale through your nose and exhale through your mouth. Allow the breath to be deep and natural.

All of the exercises begin from the standing position. The feet are slightly apart, almost shoulder width, and the knees are not locked but straight. Your weight should be evenly distributed, and your body upright but relaxed. Place your hands one over the other at the center of the chest and deepen your breath. This is the stance you will start from and return to after each exercise.

47

Exercise 4: Holding up Heaven with the Hands

1. Slowly raise your arms over your head. When you reach as high as you can, intertwine the fingers of your hands. Your palms will be facing down.

2. Rotate your hands so the palms are facing up, and firmly push up with your interlocked hands. As you push up, raise yourself slightly on your toes; just slightly so as not to lose balance. At the same time look up. Do not forget to breathe.

3. Hold this position for a few seconds, relax, and come down onto your heels. Breathe out as you slowly bring your arms down to your chest.

Exercise 5: Drawing the Bow

1. Assume the starting position as described in Exercise 4. Now, take one large step to the left. Bend your knees so you are in the riding-the-horse position. You do not have to bend them much, just make sure that you're comfortable and that your knees are soft.

2. Clench your hands into fists, and draw the bow as follows. Your right arm pulls back as if pulling the bow string, with the elbow bent and kept at the level of the shoulder if possible. But do not strain. Strength and flexibility will come with practice. At the same time, extend your left arm straight out over your left foot as if you were holding a bow. Turn your head so that you're facing left, in the direction that you would be "shooting."

3. As you extend your left arm, point your index finger at the "target," keeping the rest of the fingers clenched in a fist, and point your thumb straight upward, as if you could sight over it, like the bow itself. Remember to keep breathing while stretching the bow.

4. Relax your arms while exhaling, and bring your arms back to your center.

5. Repeat on the right side.

6. Repeat four more times.

Exercise 6: Bridging Heaven and Earth

1. Assume the beginning stance.

2. Raise the left hand up over your head, straightening your arm, and turn your palm up with a bent wrist and fingers pointed toward your head, as if you were holding up the heavens.

3. At the same time, turn your right palm toward the earth, pushing down with your right arm. Your fingers will be pointing inward with your hand slightly behind you, so your arm can be as straight down as possible. Stretch your arms apart from each other.

4. Exhale and relax, bringing your arms back to center.

5. Repeat with opposite arms. Repeat 4 more times. ✂

Exercise 7: Tiger Looking at His Tail

1. Assume the starting position.

2. Inhale while slowly moving your hands to the sides and back, palms forward and arms straight. Your hands will be at about waist high. Stretch your arms back, but do not strain yourself.

3. At the same time, turn your head to the left as far as possible—your head only, not your body— and with your eyes look for your "tail." Breathe.

4. Exhale and bring your hands back to your chest.

5. Repeat on the other side. Repeat 4 more times. ✂

Exercise 8: Swinging the Body

1. Assume the starting position.

2. Place your hands on your hips and rotate them as if you had a hula hoop around your knees. Rotate them as far as you can in every direction, with your head and feet as a sort of pivot. Do this rotation slowly 3 or 4 times.

4. Rotate in the opposite direction. Repeat 4 more times.

5. Bring your arms and hands back to center. ✂

Exercise 9: Holding Toes and Stretching Back

1. Assume the starting position.

2. Bend forward and down, and grasp your legs above the ankles with your hands behind your legs.

3. In this position, pull yourself up off of your heels with your weight more on your toes. At first this may seem difficult, and you should be careful not to lose your balance. The movement is not extreme, it may only be a slight shift in weight on your foot, but it is a stretch.

4. Now come back up and with your hands on your thighs, stretch back as if in a back bend, looking up.

5. Come back to center position. Repeat 4 times. ✂

Exercise 10: Standing on the Toes

1. Assume the starting position.

2. Extend your arms down to your sides, with hands spread out, palms to the earth. At the same time, stand up on your toes.

3. Hold this position a few seconds. Relax back to center.

4. Repeat 4 times.

Exercise 11: Angry Eyes Punching Out

1. Start at center, then step to one side, assuming the riding-a-horse position with your knees slightly bent and your weight evenly distributed.

2. Form a fist with your left hand. Make an angry face with your eyes and punch out strongly with your fist, palm down. Exhale forcefully at the same time, making a loud, angry "uh" sound with the exhalation. You are expressing anger with each punch. Be extremely forceful.

3. Repeat with the other arm. Repeat as often as you wish. Be certain to always make the angry face with your eyes with each punch.

The Essential Exercises, combined with hara breathing, which we will explore in the next chapter, should form the foundation that will lead you to be an excellent acupressurist. With technique alone you might become an acupressurist. But no technique will provide the kind of knowledge you will gain through this foundation.

These exercises will allow you to both experience chi within yourself and as a living reality. You will feel the meridians and centers of energy in your body. This will become the basis for your work on others.

5

Finding Our
Energy Centers

The energy we use and relate to in acupressure is very strong, though it is not what we in the West usually consider "strong." It cannot be observed and measured with the standard tools of physics, and it has not as yet been defined in Western scientific terms. We can refer to it as *subtle energy.*

This is not the same as "spiritual" or "mystical" energy. It is real and has been experienced, described, related, and reacted to for thousands of years. We can experience it also, but because of its subtlety, experiencing it takes practice.

While this energy is present throughout the body, it is generally most easily experienced in the body's energy centers and in our hands. These energy centers, mapped in many traditions of medicine, are best known as *chakras.* The term comes from the Hindu tradition. You may be familiar with a traditional Japanese term for one of these energy centers: the hara. In Chinese medicine this center is called the *dan tien.* In the Western tradition it is called the *solar plexus,* or "network of the sun."

By far, the best way to learn about the energy of the body is to experience it yourself. While some may have a natural sense for this, most people must train their awareness. However, experiencing this energy directly is not difficult; it is a matter of practice and attention.

BECOMING AWARE OF ENERGY

There are some basic exercises both to develop your awareness of chi and to amplify and direct its flow. Do not bypass these exercises, but do have fun with them.

Loosen Up

This exercise may not be traditional, but it is done in some of the best schools of acupressure and TCM. It is a great way to get the juices flowing, so to speak. It reduces tension easily and quickly and increases all sorts of good body processes like blood flow and oxygenation.

1. In an open area, either inside or outside, shake your body. Do not try to shake in any particular pattern, but shake each part, your hands, your arms, your shoulders, your head, your torso, hips, legs (one at a time), your feet; shake them simultaneously as much as you can. Don't shake too hard, but do wiggle and jiggle. Bounce off the floor. Shake a little, shake some more. Loosen up. That's the point of this rather silly excercise.

2. Do this for 3 to 5 minutes.

Play with an Energy Ball

Most people find this exercise fun, and it will enormously enhance the amount of energy in your hands available for you to use. It will also teach you some of the fundamentals of channeling or directing the energy flow in your body.

1. Sit in a comfortable position, either cross-legged on the floor or, preferably, on a meditation or other thick, firm cushion. If you have back problems, you may want to sit on a straight-backed chair that is short enough so your feet are flat on the floor.

2. Close your eyes and allow your breath to become full, quiet, and regular. Do not manipulate your breath, just keep your attention on it. Relax as much as you can.

3. When your breathing is regular and you feel relaxed, close your eyes and bring your hands up in front of your chest with the palms facing each other, separated by about an inch. Your arms and wrists should feel comfortably relaxed.

4. Focus your attention on the space between your hands and become aware of the energy field between them. Notice how your hands feel as you become more aware of the energy.

5. Hold this position for up to several minutes to fully experience the energy being generated between your hands. Keep breathing and stay relaxed.

6. When the energy feels strong and definite, slowly move your hands apart. As you move

55

continued on next page

your hands away from each other, imagine the energy as a soft, round ball, almost like a firm, pliable balloon that you can squeeze gently between your hands. Do this gentle squeezing and see how large a ball of energy you can hold, keeping the sense of the ball of energy between your two hands as you move them farther apart. For some, it may be the size of a tennis ball, for others as large as a basketball.

7. If you move your hands too far apart and you lose the feeling of the energy, move your hands closer together and start again.

8. Do this exercise for up to 10 minutes.

Experience a Center of Energy

This exercise is a continuation of the previous one and should be done immediately following it, because you will then have a strong sense of energy in your hands.

1. Stay in the same position and continue the same relaxed breathing.

2. Let your left hand lie relaxed in your lap or to your side, and hold your right hand over the center of your chest, with the palm of your hand toward your chest. Allow a couple of inches between your hand and your chest, and find the energy center. It may take you a few minutes to find it, but let your hand guide you. Remember

to keep your breathing centered and regular. A quiet attention to your breathing regulates the flow of energy into your hands.

3. At this point your hands are very sensitive, and you can now begin to trust them. The trick is to not think about anything, especially not what you *should* be experiencing, but rather, to allow your attention to flow toward what you are feeling and sensing in your hands. Hold this center of energy with your hand just as you did the energy ball in the previous exercise.

4. Once you have a sense of the energy in this area, focus your attention on the feeling of it, and allow your inner awareness to move more and more into this center. If it helps, imagine this center as a place of light.

5. See if you can intensify the amount of energy in this center by using your inner awareness. Some people visualize light entering their body from above and moving down into this center. Others direct their experience of inner energy through their arm and hand. Find your own way.

57

Experience the Energy

The goal in these exercises is to become secure at an almost physical level with experiencing the flows of energy in our body. I say "almost physical" because, again, this energy is not what we usually mean by physical—it is not directly observable by the usual means of measurement, such as electricity. However, this energy is experienced as physical once we learn to be aware of it. We can feel its effects: warmth, sometimes even strong heat; tingling; increased sensitivity of the skin; or a sense of lightness and "aliveness" versus heaviness and sluggishness or "deadness." Find your own words to describe it.

HARA BREATHING

The last exercise in this chapter is the foundation of acupressure. It is the fundamental beginning point and the structure for all of the work you will do; it is a practice you should adopt and use daily.

The use of chi energy in acupressure is based on the correct way of breathing. This is exactly the same as in the martial arts, the practice of t'ai chi, or in doing chi gung. It is the secret of accumulating and distributing chi.

In the West, the breathing form is usually called hara breathing, after the Japanese name for the energy center, which is just below the navel: the dan tien, or solar plexus.

Centering oneself in dan tien is crucial for the practice of acupuncture and acupressure. Without it, there can be no channeling of energy in yourself or in the person you may be working with.

The dan tien is the center where the yin and the yang energies are balanced, where the chi can be accumulated and stored, and from where the energy flows in the body and can be replenished and filled with new chi. It is a powerful technique which, with a little practice, can be very powerful and improve the quality of our daily lives, even if we never practice acupressure.

Traditional names for the hara when filled with energy are "Golden Stove," because of the sense of warmth and heat generated; "Field of Immortality;" and "Center of Vital Energy." These names may give you a sense of the quality of inner experience you will gain from developing the strength of the hara.

Try to use these images when practicing hara breathing. Using imagery promotes the appropriate physical state in the body. This relationship between mind and body has always been known in TCM, which is why the tradition uses so many imagistic terms. It is not a lack of scientific understanding, or fanciful flights of an artistic sensibility—rather, it is the recognition that the mind is a powerful and fundamental factor in regulating the function of the entire organism.

This ability of imagery to change the state of the body has only recently been discovered in Western medicine. For example, imagery has been used extensively in recent years in the field of cancer therapy and immune system dysfunctions in general. A mental image can activate various biochemical process and lead to profound physiological changes.

You will find in working on yourself or others that imagery will become a strong part of how you relate to energy. The following hara breathing exercise presents a good chance to begin. You can do the exercise in any one of three positions. All are equally appropriate. The important thing is to be relaxed. If it helps, do the relaxing sensory awareness exercises we discussed above in preparation.

59

Hara Breathing

1. Sit cross-legged as in meditation, adopt the kneeling position as in Japanese mediation, or stand.

2. Place your hands either palm up in your lap—almost as if cupping the hara—or crossed over your chest—palms toward your body. You should feel relaxed and comfortable.

3. The breathing is in 3 steps:

   • Place the tip of your tongue on the top of your mouth (palate) behind your teeth. Relax your abdominal muscles. Breathe in through your nose, slowly and evenly. Visualize your breath descending into the hara. Count 5 heartbeats as you inhale.

   • Hold the breath for about the same amount of time.

   • Dropping your tongue back into the floor of your mouth, exhale through slightly parted lips, slowly and evenly, as if making a small feather shimmer in the breeze. Contract your abdominal muscles, using them to slowly and evenly push the breath up. Visualize your breath going up and out through the top of your head. Again, count 5 heartbeats.

4. It is the inner movement of chi and not the breath itself that is important. While you are breathing in, use your inner vision—your conciousness—to direct your breath down into the hara. This the key to the entire process. It is with your con-

ciousness that you will always direct chi as you
do acupressure.

Do this exercise for at least ten minutes at a
time, at least once a day. ✂

While you are practicing hara breathing, stay aware of your
general state of tension. You should stay as relaxed as you can,
especially the abdominal muscles. The breath should not stay in
the chest area but descend into the abdomen. If you feel that this
is not happening, imagine your rib cage expanding and your
diaphragm moving down. Hold in mind this image of your
breath carrying the chi into the hara and accumulating there into
a pool of warm energy. Remember the image of the furnace.

In the exhalation, the image of the breath moving up and
out of the top of your head carries the chi from dan tien to *bei
wei,* an acupressure point also called GV 20, or "Hundred
Meeting," an important point more commonly known as the
crown chakra. (We'll get to the inital and numerical categoriza-
tions of acupressure points later in the book, when we go into
each in more detail.)

The point bei wei is the place where many traditions have
seen the energy of the universe entering the body. In acupressure,
as in cranial-sacral osteopathy, it is a very important point for
helping to balance the overall body energy.

Many practitioners of acupressure learn this form of
breathing without ever learning or doing the inner work of visualization. This is an enormous mistake. The cultivation of the
inner movement of consciousness is the key that the Chinese and

61

Japanese masters have always stressed. The importance of mastering the meditative visualization in using this form of breathing effectively cannot be stressed enough. If you work at the process of using imagery to guide energy, your acupressure will be highly effective. If you only use the techniques in an external fashion, it will not.

It will not be enough to do the exercise only a few times. This way of breathing is so fundamental that it should be consciously practiced on a daily basis until it becomes almost second nature. You should at least be able to establish it easily after a few moments of meditative centering. In this way you will be able to do acupressure easily and effectively.

6

Locating Channels
of Energy

L ike rivers and streams, the channels of essential energy flow
through and nourish the areas of the body they are near.
Large and small, each is a path of circulation and influence coursing between the various organs and between each other, forming
a network that supports, vitalizes, and regulates the body and all
of its functions.

In acupressure, we work with this flow of energy in the
meridian channels to restore balance and harmony. We must
know how to locate these channels and how to work with the
energy to enhance and harmonize its flow.

In this chapter, we'll present an overall picture of the location of the meridians and some of the most useful points. More
important than the location of the meridians, however, you will
learn how to *feel* them and recognize significant points. Through

the approach presented here, you will learn the fundamentals upon which all acupressure is based. More complex and detailed information can be gained elsewhere. The Resources chapter of the book can be consulted for further study.

MERIDIANS AND ANATOMY

The meridians—the main energy channels—can be most easily described, located, and generally understood by referring to the gross anatomy of the human body.

In China, the meridians and points were located by referring to the observable structure of the body and the common language used to describe it. A point would be described, for example, as lying against the bone of the hand on the web of flesh between the thumb and the fingers where the two bones meet.

Today, unfortunately, most English language books, and many Chinese books, have started using technical and Latin anatomical references, probably in an effort to make acupuncture more acceptable to the Western medical world. This has made a technical study of anatomy almost essential in order to read many books on acupuncture. Fortunately, there are excellent exceptions. (See the Bibliography.)

Here, we will use the traditional approach to describe the channels and points. You will learn that you can feel the meridians and points with your hands and fingers. A Chinese acupuncturist can brush his fingertips across an area of skin and unfailingly feel the exact location of the point. A Japanese practioner of shiatsu can locate the meridians by feel. As noted earlier, the practioners of acupressure were often blind, and they learned their entire skill from touch and feel only.

The division of the yin from yang areas of the body on the arms, hands, and feet can be seen more or less clearly from the change in color of the skin from the "red flesh" to the "white flesh." The red flesh, or darker colored skin, on the back of the arms, hands, and the tops of the feet visually define these parts of the body as yang areas Every area of the body is controlled by the energy flow in the meridians located in that area. Therefore, an area can be affected by points anywhere on that or any closely associated meridian. We can see, then, that because the meridians run long distances and are bilateral (in pairs on both sides of the body), an area of difficulty may be affected or helped by working on a different area from the problem one, a part at a distance, and/or on the opposite side of the body.

All of the meridians lie in grooves or between the muscles of the body. They are not found on the large, flat surfaces of muscles. Thus, you will generally find the meridians against bones. Where Western massage tends to focus on the muscles themselves, in acupressure we are primarily working around the muscles. Acupressure is not muscle massage, although shiatsu sometimes places pressure on large areas. Acupressure is still focused on the meridians and points, not on the muscles themselves.

The key points on the meridians are located at what could be seen as the most protected areas of the body: depressions at junctures between muscles, places where nerves emerge from muscles, at the base of muscles or nerves, or at creases in the skin such as the wrist fold.

All human bodies have approximately the same proportions. Therefore, measuring distances on the body—usually done in the accurate location of acupressure points—can only be done by using the body itself as the standard of measurement. For

65

example, an acupressure point may be described as being located three *cun* above the wrist fold. No matter how large or small a particular person is, this will always be an accurate measurement of location, because the cun is the width of that person's own thumb at the base of the nail. If you are not very different in size from the person you are working on, you can use your own fingers to make these measurements.

Locating the Meridians

1. Stand with your left arm stretched out straight from your side, parallel to the earth, and make a fist.

2. Turn your head to the left and sight down your arm, pointing with your index finger as if at a target, and stick your thumb straight up like a gun sight.

3. Stretch your arm out as far as you can and widen the gap between your forefinger and thumb as much as you can. You should now feel a stretch in your arm that runs from the tip of your forefinger along the arm to the shoulder.

4. With your right hand, use your fingertips to trace this "stretch line." You will find your fingers moving along a line that lies on the bone, on the red flesh of the outer arm, just off of the white flesh, which ends more or less on the top of the shoulder on the bone. Some people may find that they can feel the line run across the shoulder into their neck. Some will not.

5. As you move your fingers along your arm, notice that you are moving along the bone. See how this feels. Notice where the muscles lie as you move your fingers along your arm. Notice if you find any tender areas or spots. You may find more than one. (If you do, you can massage these points, or hold them gently.)

6. Do the same exercise on the right side, using your left hand to feel the anatomy and points. Massage or hold any sore points you find. Take as much time as you did with your left side. ✎

67

You have just experienced the location of the large intestine meridian. This yang meridian begins at the tip of the forefinger, and its chi runs down the arm (remember, the yang chi flows down from above) to and over the shoulder, neck, and jaw, and to the side of the nose.

When doing this exercise, you probably felt the location of the meridian on the surface of the arm and also felt some of the main points, which were the tender spots. This particular meridian is fairly easy to find. As you do any of these exercises, be sure to do them on each side in order to develop the sensitivity of your less developed hand.

The exercise is a part of the form known as "Drawing the Bow," one of the Eight Essential Exercises of chi gung described in Chapter 4. Other meridians are not as easy to locate, but with some practice, and by using the chi gung exercises, you will be able to feel most of the main meridians in the body. The chi gung exercises were designed to stretch and activate all of the main meridians, which is why they can be used to experience the meridians and their energy.

The descriptions of each of the meridians that follow are short and meant only to convey a brief sense of what each is about. As each is described, you should use your hands to trace and feel the course of that meridian. In this way, you will become familiar with the anatomy of the body and grow more confident in your touch.

MAIN YIN MERIDIANS

In reading the explanations that follow, refer to the accompanying figures, which will give you an anatomical sense of where the meridians lie.

Lung

The lung meridian begins at a point on the clavicle bone on the chest. It runs up the arm along the edge of the white flesh on the thumb side of the arm, ending on the end of the thumb, at the base of the nail farthest from the fingers. (See Figure 6.1.)

With your arm in front of you, palm toward you, place the palm of your other hand on the back of your arm near the wrist and curve your fingers around to the front side. Your finger tips will fall into the groove next to the bone, below the thumb, which is the channel in which the lung meridian lies. You can follow the meridian with your fingers all the way along your arm by pressing against the bone.

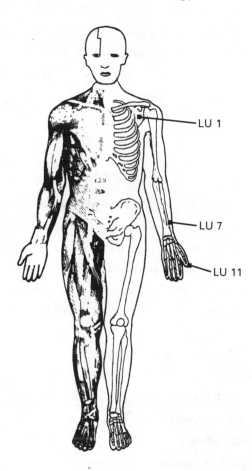

LU 1

LU 7

LU 11

69

FIGURE 6.1.   THE LUNG MERIDIAN

The function of the lung meridian is that of combining the chi from the stomach—that is, the energy produced by food—with the chi of the breath or air, to form the chi that is used by the whole body.

Imbalance of the lung meridian will create problems related to the lungs themselves, such as asthma, bronchitis, and coughs, and to certain psychological effects of loss and grief. The act of sobbing, in which the respiration becomes almost violent and jerking, demonstrates the connection of the lung meridian to this emotion of grief or anguish.

Spleen

As Figure 6.2 illustrates, the spleen meridian begins on the big toe, at the base of the nail farthest from the other toes. It runs up the side of the foot; crosses the ankle in front of the bone; and runs up the inside of the leg between the muscle and the shinbone, on the inside of the knee. It continues up the inside front of the leg and zigzags up the front of the torso, where it ends on the side of the rib cage.

With your fingers, you can trace the spleen meridian on the inside of the leg by pressing along the shinbone next to the big muscle in the lower leg. The points will probably be sore. You can look at the chart in the back of the book to see other points on this meridian.

The function of the spleen meridian is to transport and distribute around the body the chi of liquid and solid food The spleen chi also is said to "govern the blood" and "grasp the blood," and thus helps control excessive blood flow. In modern terms, the spleen is considered to include the pancreas, which explains its relationship to certain functions of digestion.

The emotion associated with this meridian is variously translated as pensiveness or anxiety. Pensiveness to the extreme

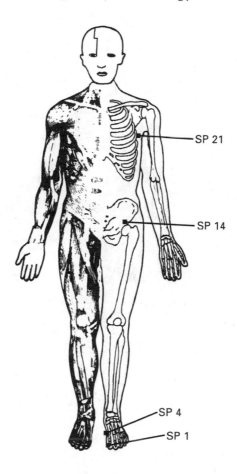

SP 21

SP 14

SP 4

SP 1

71

FIGURE 6.2.   THE SPLEEN MERIDIAN

can result in overconcern for details, restlessness from anxiety, and excessive dissatisfaction, and it may cause overcautiousness, timidity, and sleeplessness from thinking too much. Mental fatigue and memory loss are also associated with the spleen meridian.

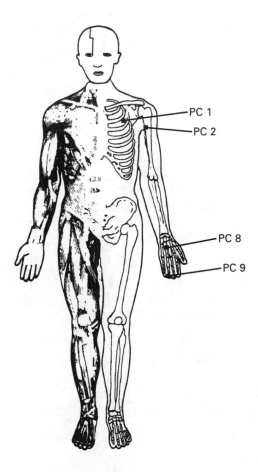

PC 1
PC 2
PC 8
PC 9

FIGURE 6.3.   THE PERICARDIUM MERIDIAN

Pericardium

This meridian, depicted in Figure 6.3, is also referred to as the circulation-sex meridian, primarily by Western acupuncturists. It will sometimes be identified by this name in some books and charts. However, the Chinese character for the meridian is the same as that for the physical pericardium and means "Heart Protector" or "Sac Enveloping the Heart."

This meridian begins where the spleen meridian ends on the torso, and it goes up the center front of the arm on the white flesh. It ends on the tip of the middle finger.

This meridian is the external protector of the heart and guards the heart energy. Because of its function, imbalances in this meridian are seen in various heart dysfunctions such as palpitations, problems with blood pressure, and pains in the region of the heart and stomach.

Pericardium Exercise

1. Stand with your hands in front of your chest.

2. Lower one hand to the side and turn the palm to the earth. At the same time, raise the other arm up and point your fingers up toward the sky.

3. Push the two hands apart. (This is one of the chi gung Eight Essential Exercises, Bridging Heaven and Earth.) The stretch that you feel on the inside of your arms is primarily along the pericardium meridian. While it may at first feel as if the entire inside of the arm is stretched, see if you can isolate with your awareness the main feel of the stretch on the center of the inside of the arm. If you can, you will probably feel the meridian all the way to the chest.

4. Do this on both sides. Remember to keep breathing while doing this exercise.

The primary emotion associated with this meridian is joy. Dysfunction can lead to depression, melancholy, and self-doubt, or to their opposites of hyperexcitement and extreme elation.

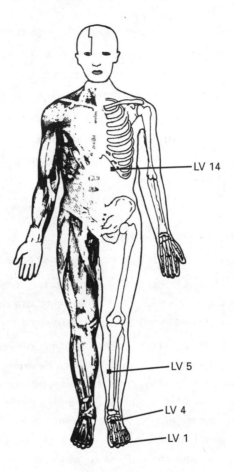

74

FIGURE 6.4. THE LIVER MERIDIAN

Liver

The liver meridian begins on the big toe on the side closest to the other toes. It runs up the leg, mostly between the other two leg yin meridians (on the inside of the leg), onto the abdominal side of the torso, and ends on the edge of the rib cage. At this point it runs internally across the chest. (See Figure 6.4.)

Ling Shu has stated, "The liver stores the blood." It has the functions of guarding against attacks and abuses from the environment, of considering plans, and of resisting disease and "evils." Thus, many illnesses can be related to the liver, presumably because of its ability to detoxify and to regulate metabolism. The liver is related to reason and cheerfulness. Both anger and depression are often related to liver dysfunction.

Heart

The heart meridian, shown in Figure 6.5, starts on the side of the upper chest and runs up the inside of the arm to the tip of the little finger.

You can feel this meridian very easily with your fingers. Hold one arm straight out in front of you with the palm up. With the thumb of your other hand, find the place where the arm bone and the big tendon to the chest intersect and put your thumb in the hollow on the arm bone. Now you can move your thumb down the inside of the bone, where the red flesh meets the white, by gently squeezing your arm between your fingers and thumb. You will feel the slight groove, and a large indentation on the inside of the elbow. You can use your thumb to follow straight on up to the tip of the little finger, following the outside edge of the finger, farthest from the other fingers.

The most ancient writers emphasized the importance of the heart as the controller of life and movement in the body. The heart stores the shen, or spirit. Ling Shu again: "The heart is the root of life and the location of change of shen." The heart thus controls the harmony of functioning of all of the other organs and parts of the body.

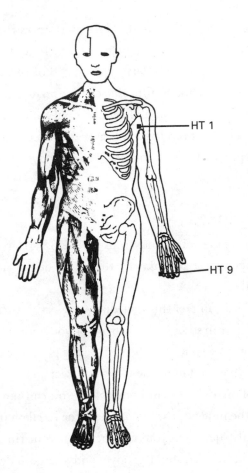

FIGURE 6.5.   THE HEART MERIDIAN

The primary emotion associated with the heart is joy, and, as with the pericardium, dysfunction will result, in depression or hyperelation.

Caution: In doing acupressure, care should be taken not to sedate or suppress the flow of chi in the heart meridian. This is the only meridian where the only action in acupressure, if taken at all, is an attempt to tonify or to increase the flow of chi.

Because of the direction of flow in this meridian, some movements of Swedish massage should not be used. Swedish massage uses pressure on the muscles in long, deep strokes, and the direction of such strokes is toward the heart in order to keep the blood flow toward the heart. If this kind of massage is done *on* the heart meridian, the direction of movement is against the natural flow of the heart meridian chi and could have a sedating action on this meridian, which is to be avoided.

Kidney

The kidney meridian starts on the center of the bottom of the foot. Bring your finger straight back along the bottom of your foot from the second (next to the big) toe and just past the pad, into the indentation. Looking at Figure 6.6, you'll see that this is the first point (KI 1) of the kidney meridian. From there, the meridian zags up into the arch of the foot and across the ankle; up the inside of the Achilles tendon (between the tendon and the bone); and up the back inside part of the leg into the groin. It continues over the abdomen and chest near the midline and ends on the clavicle bone at the top of the chest. The line up the chest area runs approximately halfway between the midline and the stomach meridian.

77

The kidneys are related to birth, growth, and reproduction. They store the reproductive chi (called *jing*), formed from the prenatal chi and postnatal chi from the five yin meridians.

The kidney controls water, stores jing, and also controls what is called the "Gate of Life," which means "the basis of life."

The flourishing of kidney chi in the early years of life leads naturally to reproduction, and as the chi wanes, it eventually leads

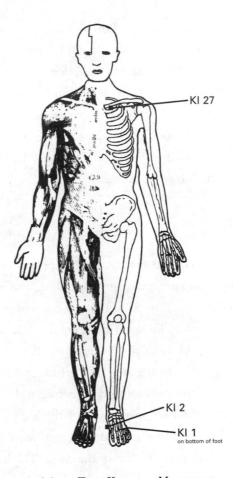

KI 27

KI 2

KI 1
on bottom of foot

78
ℒ❧

FIGURE 6.6.   THE KIDNEY MERIDIAN

to old age and sterility. So the Chinese say that at death, the kidney chi has been used up and totally depleted.

Insofar as this meridian is related to the natural processes of growth and development and aging, its dysfunction will be seen in hormonal imbalances as well as problems related to the kidneys, such as backache and stiffness in the muscles of the torso.

The dominant emotion related to the kidneys is fear and apprehension. Imbalance can lead to pessimism, or to being a workaholic.

Conception Vessel

The conception vessel is the second of the two extra meridians that have their own points. In Chinese medicine it begins at the center of the perineum, halfway between the genitals and the anus. From there it rises up the midline of the front of the body, ending below the lower lip. (See Figure 6.7.)

However, in the mystical Taoist tradition, the energy of the conception vessel is conceived as running down the front of the body as a continuation of the circular energy flow in the governing vessel. (More on this, and the flow of energy in the great central channel, below.) To find the conception vessel, place the fingers of one hand on the center of the breastbone, across the top of your chest, and gently trace the meridian down the center line of the body, feeling for any tender spots. You will most likely find points on the bones of the chest area that are quite tender. These will be points on the conception vessel.

The conception vessel is the most yin of the yin meridians and is called the "sea" of the yin meridians. This meridian controls the yin meridians of the body. It is the root of conception in the woman. The points on this meridian are traditionally related to the regulation of various genitourinary and digestive functions in both men and women. However, in acupressure we put a great deal of emphasis upon this meridian in relation to its nourishing and nurturing function for the whole person.

79

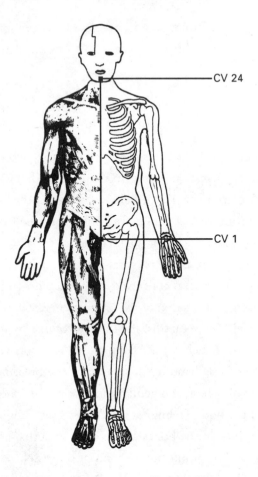

CV 24

CV 1

FIGURE 6.7.   THE CONCEPTION VESSEL MERIDIAN

This meridian is also significant as a continuation of the flow of the great central channel on the front of the body—flow that regulates the energy in the entire body.

Perhaps you have begun to see the complexity of the meridian system, but also some of its order and simplicity, as well. While the web of channels has been described as separate entities, we can begin to see that these are parts of the whole flow of energy through the entire body, creating a single unity of the body-mind.

While the complexity of this system can be studied for a lifetime, the aim here is to outline the system in such a way that it is approachable and useful even without a detailed knowledge of the meridians. The keys to doing this are both a good overview and, especially, a growing sensitivity and respect for the subtle flow of the chi that permeates and is the foundation for the life of the body.

MAIN YANG MERIDIANS

An exercise presented earlier led through the steps that would enable you to experience the location of the large intestine meridian. Let's begin our study of the main yang meridians with that.

Large Intestine

The large intestine meridian, illustrated in Figures 6.8a and b, begins at the end of the index finger (the point is designated as LI 1) and runs along the arm, across the shoulder and neck to the face, where it ends at the edge of the nose. Remember, this meridian is bilateral (on both sides of the body). At this point the stomach meridian begins, continuing to channel yang energy down the body to the feet.

The most general description of the function of the large intestine meridian is "the transmission and drainage of the dregs." This description is true of both physical and emotional dregs, the

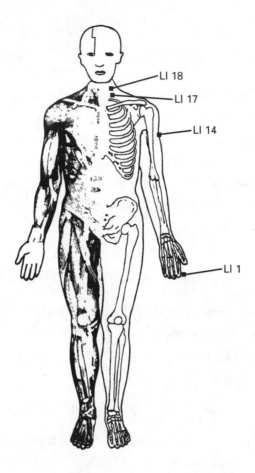

FIGURE 6.8a.   THE LARGE INTESTINE MERIDIAN
Front View

end product of ingestion and digestion, the final waste material that must be gotten rid of.

When the energy of this meridian is weak, a possible consequence is constipation, nasal congestion, bronchial congestion, and malfunctioning or weakness in the lower part of the body in

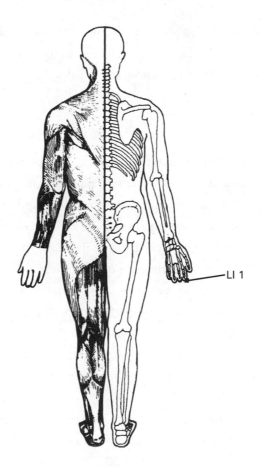

LI 1

FIGURE 6.8b.
Back View

general. For the individual experiencing the meridian's weakness, there may be a lack of determination, a tendency to disappointment, and overdependency. On the other hand, if there is excessive energy in the large intestine meridian, there will be a propensity to overeat, pain or stiffness in the area of the meridian, and headache, in addition to the physical conditions cited above. Psychologically, there will be a perpetual dissatisfaction and sense of having no friend in whom to confide.

Stomach

The stomach meridian begins at the end of the large intestine meridian at the side of the nose and goes up to below the eye (on an imaginary line straight down from the pupil) before descending down the body (some authorities believe it actually starts below the eye and descends). The meridian then goes down the neck onto the chest, running down an imaginary line that runs through the nipple; then down the torso; down the outside front of the leg; and along the top of the foot, where it ends at the tip of the second toe.

Look at Figure 6.9, the stomach meridian. Trace the meridian on your body with your hand. Be sure to do this with both hands. Do this slowly and feel for any sensitive spots.

The stomach is called in Chinese medicine "the sea of water and nourishment and the controller of the rotting and ripening of liquid and solid food." The "rotting and ripening" of food in the stomach produces the chi used to nourish all of the organs of the body. Without this nourishment, the rest of the body would not function. Again, there is an emotional component to the function of this meridian.

Various stomach and gastric disorders are the result of excessive or weak stomach chi. Eating disorders are also related, including psychologically based overeating. There can be a tendency to think too much, be nervous about details, have frustration, and overwork.

84

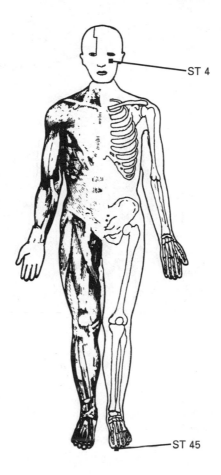

ST 4

ST 45

85

FIGURE 6.9.   THE STOMACH MERIDIAN

Triple Warmer

Shown in Figures 6.10a and b, the name of this meridian refers to the three "warmers," or centers of energy in the body as seen by the Chinese. The meridian begins at the tip of the third (or ring) finger. It runs along the back of the hand to the center of the back of the wrist; along the center of the back of the arm

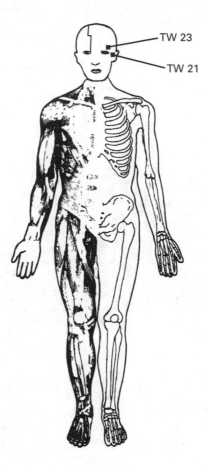

TW 23

TW 21

86

FIGURE 6.10a.   THE TRIPLE WARMER MERIDIAN
Front View

between the other two upper yang meridians; across the shoulder
and up the neck to points around the ear; and it ends at the outer
corner of the eyebrow.

Follow the course of this meridian with your hands. It is easy
to find on the arm, between the two bones of the arm between the
wrist and elbow and between the elbow and shoulder. If you stand

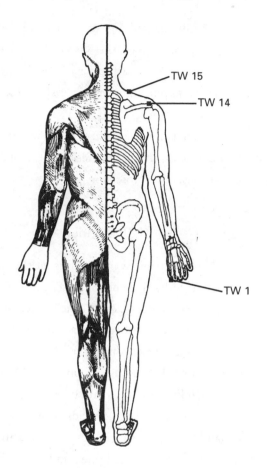

TW 15

TW 14

TW 1

87

FIGURE 6.10b.
Back View

with the palm of your hand to the front, it is exactly against the bone on the back side of the arm. Often, you will find sore points along this meridian in the area of the upper arm.

Each of the three warmers has its own special function. However, in general, the function of the triple warmer meridian is the distribution and circulation of the nourishing chi and fluids generated by the intake and digestion of food and liquid. In so doing, it is the protector of the yin and yang organs. Thus, Zhangshi Leijing says, "The triple warmer is the external protector of the *zang* and *fu* [yin and yang organs] . . . like the wall protecting the Imperial Palace."

Imbalances in this meridian can result in extra sensitivity to heat, cold, or dampness and a constriction of mental attitude leading to overcautiousness or obsessions.

Gall Bladder

Beginning where the triple warmer ends (at the outer corner of the eye) the gall bladder meridian zigzags across the head, down the neck, outside of the torso, down the center of the outside of the leg (between the two other lower yang meridians), in front of the knobby bone on the outside of the ankle, and it ends at the tip of the fourth toe. Thus, it continues the channeling of yang energy. (See Figures 6.11a and b.)

You can easily locate this meridian on your leg by feeling with your hands along the outside of the bone in the upper leg and for the indent between the bone and the muscle on the outside of the lower leg. You may find sore points, since the gall bladder meridian will reveal body toxicity.

The gall bladder meridian has the function of purifying the yang energy and storing pure chi, thus the Chinese say it controls the function of making plans and judgements. As Su Wen put it, "The gall bladder is the true and upright official who excels in making decisions." It distributes nutrients and balances the total energy.

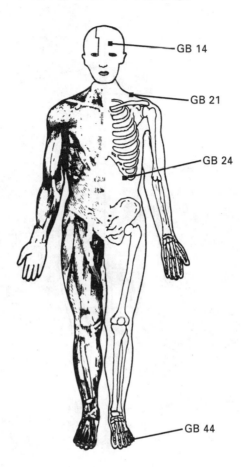

GB 14

GB 21

GB 24

GB 44

89

FIGURE 6.11a.   THE GALL BLADDER MERIDIAN
Front View

Imbalance is related to problems of poor nutrition, sleep-lessness, and the fatigue related to having strained nerves, assuming too much responsibility, and being impatient. As with the liver, anger can be excessive and uncontrolled.

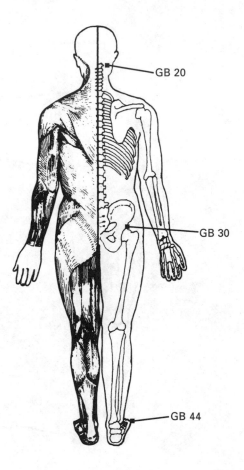

FIGURE 6.11b.
Back View

Small Intestine

The small intestine meridian starts at the tip of the little finger and runs down the back of the hand at edge of the red flesh. When the arm is up and the thumb is toward the body, the course of the meridian continues down the outside back of the arm; over

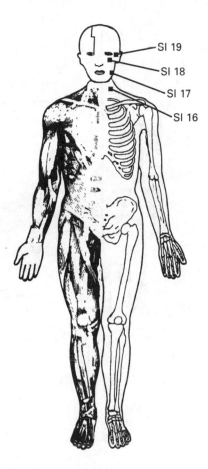

SI 19
SI 18
SI 17
SI 16

91

FIGURE 6.12a.   THE SMALL INTESTINE
Front View

the shoulder, neck, and face; and ends at the front of the ear. Although only some charts show it, the small intestine meridian connects with the first point of the bladder meridian at the inside corner of the eye as it goes across the face. The two channels connect here to continue the downward flow of the yin chi. (See Figures 6.12a and b.)

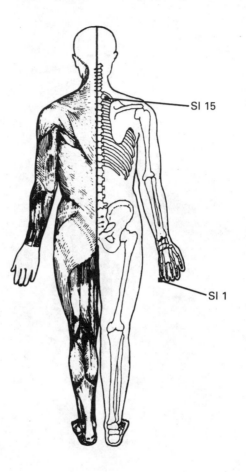

FIGURE 6.12b.
Back View

The meridian is easily felt in the forearm. Place the palm of your hand on the underside (yin) of your arm and press the tips of your fingers against the topside of your arm, into the groove between the bone and the muscle. Your wrist must be relaxed or the muscle will be too tense to allow the fingers into the groove. Once again, you may find tender points. You can follow this meridian by feel alone to the elbow, where a key point is in the deep indentation between the two bones. By now you can probably follow the meridian by feel, along the edge of the red flesh to the shoulder.

The Chinese conception of the small intestine's function is, to a certain extent, consistent with that of Western medicine. It is seen continuing the process of digestion started by the stomach. It not only controls the transformation of matter, but it also separates the pure from the impure.

Difficulties resulting from an imbalance are usually related to poor nutrition due to digestive problems, or problems in the abdominal area. Weakness can lead to being overwhelmed by deep inner sadness or emotional shock and oversensitivity to small things. An excess can result in holding everything inside, overworking, and experiencing headaches.

93

Bladder

This meridian begins at the inner corner of the eye. It goes up over the top of the head in a more or less straight line, a little to the side of the center; down the neck, where it splits into two parallel courses going straight down the back, across the buttocks; and becomes single again as it descends the backside of the leg, on the outside of the Achilles tendon. It then runs along the outside of the foot at the edge of the red flesh to the tip of the little toe. (See Figures 6.13a and b.)

The easiest place to find part of this meridian is on your head. Place the palms of your hands above your ears so your fingers come together at the top of your head. Now pull your fingers away from the centerline of the head toward the sides until you

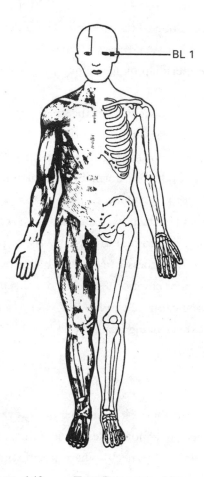

BL 1

94

FIGURE 6.13a.   THE BLADDER MERIDIAN
Front View

can feel a slight indention in the skull. This is the channel of the bladder meridian.

The rest of the meridian can only be found on another person, because it runs so close to the spine. As this meridian is very important in acupressure, we will come back to it in more detail later.

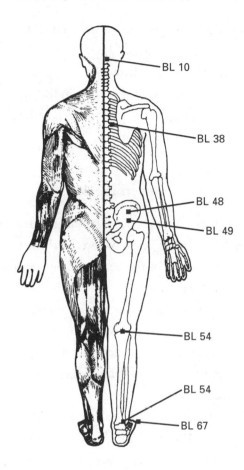

FIGURE 6.13b.
Back View

The bladder meridian is related to urine and sweat, which are the eliminative fluids of the body. However, its stronger significance is in how it differs from all of the other meridians. The bladder meridian has associated points related to all of the other meridians. These points, called *yu,* lie on that portion of the meridian that is parallel to the spine. The yu points can be used to balance the associated meridian. They are therefore very important in acupressure.

Besides urinary problems, those with apprehension or fear will have prominent muscular tension in the shoulders, back, and upper legs. They might also have migraine headaches, strained nerves, or nervous exhaustion.

Governing Vessel

One of the eight "extra meridians," the governing vessel, shown in Figures 6.14a and b, lies between the tip of the coccyx, along the spine, over the top of the head, and descends to the upper lip and gum. The flow is up.

The rule that yin flows up and yang flows down applies to the main meridians only. It does not apply to the "strange flows." They are conceived as not having direction, except for the great central or regulator channel—the conception vessel and the governing vessel.

There is a seeming discrepancy about the direction of flow in the various traditions. In most books on Chinese medicine, the flow of both the conception vessel and the governing vessel is described as up. It is thought that with aging, the general focus of energy in the body moves from the area of the lower energy centers to the head, signifying the more spiritual concerns of older age.

However, in the mystical Taoist tradition, the direction of flow of all of the strange flows is up the back and down the front. This means that the direction of flow of the great central channel is exactly the opposite of the main meridians on the front and back of the body.

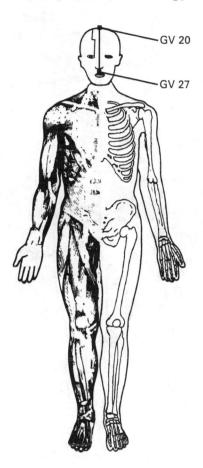

FIGURE 6.14a.   THE GOVERNING VESSEL
Front View

One explanation for the difference among the traditions has to do with the typical direction of the flow in those who do not maintain a spiritual practice. Those who are seekers of the tao (the Way), according to this explanation, found in their practice of acupressure that directing the flow of chi energy up the back and down the front was a powerful way of replenishing the entire

97

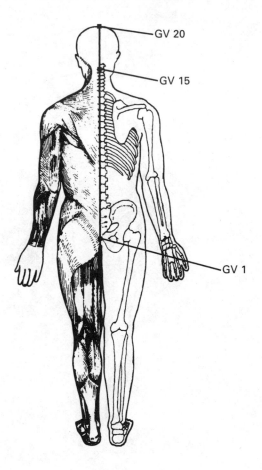

FIGURE 6.14b.
Back View

body energy as the spiritual consciousness developed. This was done through either meditation or "exoteric" acupressure.

In practice, it has been found that working with the great central channel as a flow of energy that goes up the back and down the front is useful in encouraging a more continuous flow of chi and for releasing various blockages and places of stagnation.

The governing vessel is the most yang of the yang meridians and is said to rule or regulate all of the yang meridians. The function of this meridian is to unite the yang chi of the entire body. It also connects to the conception vessel, the "sea of the yin meridians," in the mouth. In doing meditation or chi gung, the tip of the tongue is placed against the roof of the mouth against the teeth, the last point of the governing vessel. Thus, the yin and yang flow of the central meridians is united.

99

PART III

USING YOUR HANDS
IN ACUPRESSURE

7

Developing
Sensitivity

How do we translate the understanding of the meridians and their functions into working on the body with our hands? This, after all, is the work of acupressure.

In acupressure, there are several ways that the hands can be used. Basic to all of them is developing sensitivity. Specific techniques of using the fingers and hands will be covered elsewhere. But if you lack sensitivity to the natural feel and rhythm of the body—your own or someone else's—you will more than likely be intrusive rather than helpful, and neither you nor another person will feel more relaxed or helped by acupressure.

We will begin by doing some exercises to develop awareness and sensitivity of our hands. A discussion of the what, why, and how we move our hands or fingers will accompany each exercise. In this way, you can begin to acquire the sensitivity that will lead to an easy flow of gently working on another person.

Some of the techniques described in Chinese and Japanese books on meridian-based therapeutic massage (acupressure) are subtle variations of a few basics and are particularly useful to the medical practitioner of acupressure. They can be found especially in books on Tui Na (a form of Chinese massage) and Amma (a form of Japanese massage). We will not go into them here, nor will we explore the specific techniques of shiatsu. They are best learned in practice from a practitioner.

MERIDIANS AND SORE POINTS

In exploring a section of a meridian, you will feel it from both inside and out. When you work on yourself, you can easily regulate the amount of pressure you exert before there is any pain. When you work on another person, you must regulate the pressure as best you can from this knowledge of having worked on yourself, as well as asking for verbal feedback.

You will invariably find that certain places were more tender than others. You can feel tender places with the tips of your fingers as well as from the inside because they are sore. These places will feel harder, like little knots or pebbles, perhaps, or sometimes colder or hotter than the surrounding area. Sometimes, they will just feel different—flat, smushy, or dead. If you do not feel any of these differences yet, you will as you gain experience with practice. For now, it is enough to feel from the inside and recognize the lack of uniformity—there are subtle changes in the meridians, which are caused by the flow or stagnation of the chi energy.

Exploring a Meridian

Remember, before doing any exercise in this book, first do hara breathing, as discussed in Chapter 5, to build up the chi in your body and hands and to relax and center your breathing.

1. Sit on the floor or on a pad with your knees bent and feet on the floor so that you can easily put your hands on the lower part of your legs from the ankle up to the knees. Do this exercise first on one leg and then the other.

2. Place the fingers of one hand on the tendon on the back of the ankle, in the center of the leg. Slowly press in and then release the pressure.

3. Move your fingers up slightly, an inch or so, and repeat. Gently press in with your fingers and then release the pressure. Do this slowly. If there is soreness, do not press too hard. Continue pressing, moving slowly up the leg. You will feel as fingers move off the tendon and onto the leg bone. Eventually, as you move your fingers up the leg bone, you will feel that you are in a groove between two muscles, and finally, as you come to the back of the knee, your fingers will be in a deep impression between two tendons.

4. As you move your fingers up, pressing, notice how hard you press before it becomes sore. Note the feel of the skin and how much flesh there is (or the lack of it) between the skin and the bone. Notice if there are sore points and where they are.

continued on next page

105

5. After doing this on both sides, start again at the back of the ankle, but this time use both hands and slide your fingers up the muscle just to each side of the centerline. See how this feels. Notice if there are sore points or a generalized tenderness. Again, observe how much pressure you exert before there is soreness. ✂

Feeling Sore Points, Part 1

1. Hold one arm with the elbow bent and the palm of your hand facing the upper part of your chest.

2. Curl the fingers of your other hand around to the outer side of the arm with the tips of your fingers on the centerline and your thumb flat against the inside of the arm. Start at the back of the wrist, and slowly press your fingers into the center imaginary line running down your arm toward your elbow.

3. Release the pressure and move your fingers an inch or so down. You will find that your fingers are now between the two bones of the arm when you press them in. Gently and slowly press in, feeling for the differences and any sore points. Again, notice how much pressure you exert before there is soreness or pain. Notice where the sorest points are. ✂

Feeling Sore Points, Part 2

1. In a sitting position, place the tips of the first (index) fingers on the top of the bones that run across the top of the chest. Place them just on each side of the centerline.

2. Press down very gently, in the direction of your feet (not in the direction of the lungs). Stay on top of the bones, and slowly press in and release. Then move your fingers slightly farther apart and press gently again.

3. In this manner, feel the entire top of the bones to the shoulders. You will probably find many sore points. Be very gentle. Do not press too hard, but do notice where they are. See if you can feel the indentations along the bones as you push down.

4. Now start over at the centerline, and when you come to the first sore point, stop.

5. Gently press the sore point with each of your two fingers (assuming the soreness is on both sides; if not, work on the sore side). Press just until it begins to hurt, but not so much that you can't tolerate the pain. (Do not be a martyr here. Respect the body's pain signals.)

6. Hold the pressure for 10 to 15 seconds and then release the pressure quickly.

7. Repeat this a second time, in the same place. Press, hold, and release. Then do this a third

107

continued on next page

time and perhaps a fourth. Notice if the soreness reduces or disappears. Then, notice if
you have to exert more pressure the third or
fourth time before you feel the same amount
of soreness. ✄

In these two soreness exercises, you have begun to learn
how to find the location of the meridian channels by feel alone
and also just how sensitive some places on the body can be.
Further, you have experienced the sensitivity of your fingers and
observed that you can feel differences in the quality of "tone" of
different places.

Finally, you have learned a very basic technique of acupressure. You have discovered how to exert one kind of pressure
on the meridians and how that changes the flow of energy. When
an area is sore, it is due to blockage in the channel of the flow of
energy. And when the soreness begins to subside, it is because the
blockage has been reduced and the energy is flowing in a more
balanced manner.

As you gain experience in working on yourself and others,
you will discover that you can feel the blockage in an area as muscle tension, or knots or hardness, with your fingers. Your fingers
will tell you when a blockage has been released. That's because
the area will feel more like the surrounding area.

108

SENSITIVITY EXERCISES

The following exercises will develop your sensitivity skills.

Exercise with a Dime

This is an exercise used by old-time osteopathic physicians-in-training to develop sensitivity of touch. By doing this often, you can build up this sensitivity so you can feel with considerable skill the quality of the tension, knots, and so forth under the skin. Over time, by doing this exercise often, you should be able to build up the number of layers of paper obscuring the dime.

1. Place a dime on the skin of your thigh under a layer of the fabric of your pants.

2. Place a piece of tissue paper over your pant leg, covering it and the dime.

3. Run your fingertips lightly over the area and see if you can feel the shape of the dime.

4. Add a second sheet of paper. Find the dime again by feel. (Close your eyes.) Do this with each hand, using a light touch with your fingertips.

5. Keep adding sheets of paper until you are unable to feel the dime. If you find that it is too easy to do this because of the extreme flexibility of the tissue paper, try use typing paper instead.

Exercise with Another Person

Now you are going to use the skills you have begun to develop on another person.

1. Have the person either lie with his or her back up on a pad or mat on the floor, or on a massage table. Do not use a bed, unless it is a firm futon on a rigid support frame. Alternately, the person could sit on a straight-back chair, straddling and facing the back of the chair and using a pillow to rest the head on. In whatever position, the person should be comfortable and relaxed. If lying on the stomach puts a strain on the back, put a cushion under the person's stomach and another under the feet so the legs are slightly bent at the knee. They may be either clothed in a light shirt or not. But you want to be able to feel the spinal column unhindered.

2. Gently place both of your hands on the person's upper back, over the lungs. Just rest them there. Do not do anything.

3. Close your eyes, relax, and keep breathing. Focus your attention on the other person's breathing and stay focused on it for several minutes. Notice if your breathing and the other person's become synchronized. Some people find that it does. If it does not, don't worry. It just sometimes happens.

4. Keeping your eyes closed, find the person's spinal column with the tips of the fingers of both hands. Feel up and down the spine, feeling the bones and the spaces between them. Do not

use anything except a gentle touch. You are exploring the feel of the anatomy of the spine.

5. After you sense that you have become familiar with the spinal column, slide your fingers with gentle pressure out, away from the spine, until you feel a muscular band running parallel to the spine. See if you can follow this band with your fingers, slowly up and down the back.

6. Try the other side of the spine. While slowly sliding your fingers gently up and down, notice if you feel any bumps or knots. Just notice, do not do anything.

7. After you feel comfortably familiar with the person's back, place your fingertips in the spaces on one side of the spine. (You explored the top of the spinal column first.) Move your hands along the spine, feeling first one side of the spinal column, then the other.

8. Now, starting at the top of the spine, on the side closest to you (unless you are directly behind the person), place the first two fingers of one hand in the space to the side of and between two vertebra. Let your other hand rest gently on the lower part of the spine. Press slowly but more forcefully down at the side of the spine. Release the pressure and move your fingers down to the next space. As you do this, you will undoubtedly find that the person has sore places. Ask for verbal feedback. If the person reports soreness or tenderness, see if you can feel any difference

111

continued on next page

> between the sore place and one that was not. Use your fingertips to do this.
>
> 9. Do the same thing on the other side of the spine, gently pressing down in the spaces between the vertebra from the neck down. Remember to ask for verbal feedback and to notice the amount of pressure you are exerting before the person reports soreness. ✂

A note of caution: **Do not ever exert downward pressure directly on the spinal column!** This is very dangerous, and it could lead to severe injury.

112

FEELING THE POINTS

Asking for verbal feedback whenever you are exerting pressure is very important. An extremely experienced acupressurist may rarely ask for feedback, however, this is the only way to learn about the use of pressure while at the same time respecting the comfort and limits of the person you're working on.

Finally, many acupressurists work to be able to feel the "pulse" of a point. This is not a precisely accurate description of what is actually felt, but it is the closest term. In essence, the acupressurist can feel the energy flow in the meridian at the key points with the fingertips.

Some acupuncturists say that a point can be visually detected by the color of the skin, such as a shiny or pale spot or a freckle. Some say the skin will be rough or smooth, or hot or cold, in relation to the area around it. With practice you may be able to identify the location of points in this manner.

Some acupressurists, however, locate points anatomically, as we have described, and then feel the energy in the point with their fingers. This is done by lightly touching the point with the fingertip and holding it while feeling for its "pulse" or "tingle."

You can try this by picking an easily located point (not on the wrist, where you might just find a real pulse), perhaps on the back of the arm. Run your fingers along a meridian until you find a sore point, then see if you can feel the energy in the point. Keep your eyes closed and place the tip of your finger lightly on the point. See if you can feel it.

When the strong pulse is finally felt, it is said that the point has opened up. The blocked chi has been released.

Only with practice will you know if you can develop this sensitivity. If you cannot feel the energy points in this way, do not worry. There are other ways to find out if the blockage in a point has been released. These will be covered.

8

Knowing
What to Do

The term *acupressure* includes a very wide variety of body therapies and techniques, most of which are rooted in TCM. Some of the forms include shiatsu, Tui Na, Amma, and other Chinese and Japanese skills. In North America, other forms exist, sometimes unique to the West, called by such names as Jin Shin, Jin Shin Do, Jin Shin Jitsu, Touch for Health, and reflexology.

For the purpose of learning and developing skills, we can divide acupressure into two general styles: traditional acupressure, and subtle acupressure. In China or Japan these styles would probably not be recognized as specifically different from each other, but because of the way acupressure has developed in North America, they have become very obviously different in approach.

1. Traditional acupressure uses the basic techniques of Chinese and Japanese masotherapy and is based on the theory of TCM.

2. Subtle acupressure, primarily developed and used in
   the United States, is based on a more eclectic theory.

The second style of acupressure naturally evolved out of the first. It style has been influenced by some of the body therapies of the West, including traditional osteopathy and by the popular "energy work" developed in the last half century. This second style would include such schools as reiki, Jin Shin Do, Touch for Health, reflexology, and auric healing. Some of the second group does not use meridian theory at all.

This book focuses on the more traditional forms of acupressure. The exception will be the technique of holding points used extensively in Jin Shin Do, which is explained in some depth.

TECHNIQUES

The acupressure meridians and points can be stimulated in many ways by the fingers and hands. Each has variations depending on the particular school or style. The basics, however, are used by all of the styles.

Pressure

In acupressure, as distinct from acupuncture, the points and meridians are stimulated or calmed by the use of pressure in the general area of the points, rather than the acute and direct stimulation created by the insertion of a needle. Pressure is most often exerted with the palm of the hand, thumbs, and fingertips. Occasionally, an acupressurist will use the knuckle of a finger, the point of the elbow, or the entire side of the forearm.

This use of pressure has some clear advantages:

- Knowing the precise location of points is not necessary in order to apply pressure to them. While knowledge of the location of the meridians is necessary, the location of the points can be determined through both feel and verbal feedback. But, stimulation of the points can be done through pressure applied to a general area.
- Energy in the meridians can be channeled with the hands. As the hands have a powerful energy field of their own, they can add a quality that is not available in acupuncture. (In acupuncture, the needle may be turned or vibrated to add additional stimulation to the point.)
- Another advantage of acupressure is the ability to calm the tension in the area of the point by the pressure-release method. This makes stimulation of the points more effective. (Note: some acupuncturists—especially classically trained Chinese acupuncturists—use acupressure prior to an acupuncture treatment for just this purpose.)

Thumbs

By using the thumbs, you can exert fairly heavy pressure on the area of a single point. Considerably more pressure can be exerted using the thumb instead of a fingertip. Using the thumbs to exert direct pressure on the points and meridians is particularly helpful on the back, head, forearms, and lower legs. Try using your thumbs to press points below the back of the skull, on the bony ridge.

117

The thumbs can be used to rub along a meridian or to exert a squeezing pressure on two sides of an area. Try this on your thigh, squeezing the area along the stomach meridian, on the centerline of the leg. You will find you can exert considerable pressure in this manner. This technique can be used very easily to help relieve blockage of the flow of chi in a meridian.

Palms of the Hands

The palms of the hands can be used in a variety of ways. The most common use is to exert even pressure over a large area. This can be done with one hand, two hands in different areas, the two hands next to each other, or with the second hand placed on top of the first in order to exert stronger pressure.

Try these ways now, on your own leg. And if you have a friend handy, practice on his or her back, and ask for verbal feedback.

This use of the hands can have a variety of effects.

Placing the hands lightly on one part of the body, for example, can be very calming. Resting them at two different parts can help balance the energy between these two areas.

Using these styles with pressure can help relax tense areas of the body. It can also directly stimulate a meridian or several points at a time. This is particularly true on the legs and on the back.

Tips of the Fingers

For most of us, the sensitivity of the index finger is well-developed. Some will actually be able to feel the energy points with the index finger.

The index finger is often used to stimulate a single point on a meridian. If more pressure is needed, the end of the middle finger can be placed on the nail of the index finger of the same hand. This tends to stabilize the index finger and allow for more exertion of pressure without straining the finger.

Using the Fingers Together

There are many occasions in the practice of acupressure when you will want to work on the points on the back, the backside of the legs, or the base of the head in a slow, methodical manner. The key to doing this is to have the person you are working on lie on their back with your hands under them.

In this style, the hand is gently slid under the person (who is lying on his or her back on a pad or padded table), and the fingers are curved upward, so the tips are pressing against the body. The weight of the person exerts the pressure.

119

With the table supporting the hand of the acupressurist, considerable pressure can be placed on a point or group of points for several minutes or longer without fatigue. This is one of the most important positions for the hands in acupressure.

Fingertip Exercise

The focus should be one of a relaxed sensation of energy flow in the hara, and perhaps through your hands as well. If you try to focus on your fingers, you risk the chance of losing the relaxed breathing and the flow of energy from your center.

1. Have a partner lie on his or her back on a pad or table.

continued on next page

2. After you both have relaxed and your breathing is centered, slide one hand, palm up, under the person's lower back until the tips of your fingers touch the spine. Slide the other hand similarly under the chest area of the back.

3. One at a time, pull your hand back from the spine until you can feel the spaces next to it—the channel through which the energy of the inner bladder meridian runs.

4. Press up with the ends of your fingers while at the same time curving them and sliding your hand back toward the spine about an inch or two. This movement should leave your fingers comfortably curved up, with their ends pushing into the person's back. Your hand should be relaxed, and the weight of the subject should provide all of the pressure. No effort is needed to press the points when your hands are positioned in this manner.

5. Do this with each hand, so that you are holding points with both hands simultaneously. Keep your eyes closed and focus your attention on your hara and breathing. ✄

120

The Elbow

The end of the elbow can be used to exert pressure on points where it might be difficult to exert enough pressure. This would include the lower back and the buttocks. When using the elbow, be sure to press slowly so as to not cause pain. The other hand is used to hold the wrist of the bent arm you are using, which stabilizes the arm as you press down with the elbow point. You should try this on yourself. Use the center meridian of the upper leg to practice the amount of pressure you can exert with your elbow.

Rubbing and Stroking

This technique can be used to stimulate a point very effectively. Only the fingers or palm of the hand is used.

The general area of a specific point is briskly rubbed in order to stimulate it. This will produce a warming effect and activate the tissues around the point. It gently stimulates the skin and the underlying tissue.

Stroking can be applied to several points in an area at once. In this way a large area such as the back or thigh can be worked on easily.

To activate the flow of energy in a meridian, you can stroke in the natural direction of the energy flow in that particular meridian. This is a very effective technique. The pressure can range from almost feather light to moderately heavy, depending on the area of the body and the effect desired.

Caution: Feather-light touch with the fingertips can be extremely energizing and invigorating. However, some people find it very uncomfortable, particularly in certain areas of the body such as the feet. On the other hand, in combination with patting (see following section) on the points on the bladder meridian, feather-light stroking is very effective to stimulate development and coordination in children with slow or dysfunctional motor development. Do not do feather-light stroking

121

without great consciousness of why you are doing it and what the immediate effect is on the other person.

Patting

Patting with the fingers or palms can be done on many parts of the body and has a stimulating effect. It is particularly effective in such areas as the head, back, buttocks, and thighs.

Patting must be done with a soft and elastic wrist, using your shoulders and not your wrists to create the patting motion. The fingers, if used, should be slightly bent, to give a little spring when they actually strike the body.

Patting with the center of the palm is often done on the back area. The fingers are held straight and close together so the palm of the hand is like a shallow cup, which is used to pat the body.

Caution should be used when it comes to patting the abdominal area or chest. These areas are very tender and sensitive. Unless there is a very good reason, it should probably be avoided.

Some acupressurists pat the bottoms of the feet. This has the effect of stimulating the areas that are associated, in Touch for Health and osteopathy with all of the various organs of the body. (There are charts showing the map of the bottom of the feet.) However, some people are very sensitive here, and pressing and rubbing are probably more appropriate for most on the feet themselves.

Bending, Stretching, and Rotating

While we usually associate these methods with shiatsu, each can be used judiciously in the course of a typical acupressure treatment.

122

Bending of the arms and legs can be done using the natural flexibility and direction of bends as a guide. For example, with the subject lying on his or her back, the leg can be bent at the hip and knee, bringing the knee toward the chest area. The person should be instructed to relax and let the acupressurist do the lifting and bending.

The acupressurist must use both arms and expect to carry the weight of the leg. If the subject lends "help" to the acupressurist, the movement can be repeated several times with a reminder to relax. The acupressurist then pushes just a little bit harder in the direction of the chest to increase the bend slightly beyond normal. Bending promotes muscle relaxation in the area, general relaxation, and can help release muscle and tendon tension created by overuse or past minor injury.

Bending should always be done slowly, gently, and in the direction of the natural bends of the limbs.

Verbal feedback should be elicited, and care should be taken that an old injury to a joint is respected. While bending can help release excessive tension, it cannot release scar tissue that may have built up in the past.

Rotating is a natural extension of the method of bending. For example, the arm can be rotated at the elbow. With the person sitting comfortably with his or her arm hanging at the side, the acupressurist will lift the upper arm away from the body in such a way that the forearm hangs in a relaxed position. The arm can then be rotated in a circular motion, slowly and gently, not exceeding its natural range of motion. Again, this can be very relaxing and improve the range of motion due to tension or past injury.

The head can be rotated carefully, both from side to side and from front to back (with the person lying down), bending

123

and stretching the neck muscles. Again, caution should be used and verbal feedback invited so as to not cause any pain. This method can give great relief to neck and shoulder tension.

Stretching

Stretches can be done in many parts of the body. The first precaution is to be certain that the stretch is in the natural direction of the limb and the muscles. The second precaution is to hold the limb in the appropriate place, so as not to do any injury to the connective tissue and joints. For example, the leg is stretched away from the torso by holding the lower leg—not the foot—in both hands. Holding the foot and then pulling could injure the ankle. Likewise, the lower arm—not the hand—is held in an arm stretch.

Two stretches that are very relaxing to most people are the neck stretch and the shoulder/neck stretch.

The neck stretch is achieved with the person lying on her or his back and the acupressurist lifting and holding the person's head in both hands about an inch off the pad. With the hands firmly holding the head at the base of the skull, the head is pulled away from the body by the acupressurist, who leans backward. A very nice stretch is achieved in this manner.

The neck/shoulder stretch can be done in two ways.

With the person sitting firmly on a mat, the acupressurist, standing behind the person, places his or her forearms near the elbow on the middle points of each shoulder. By leaning, the acupressurist can exert considerable pressure on one or the other shoulder, rocking it from side to side or on both shoulders at the same time. This gives an excellent stretch to this area.

124

The second way to give the stretch is with the person lying on his or her back on a mat or table. The acupressurist places both hands on the shoulders, cupping the shoulder with the hand. With straight arms, the acupressurist leans forward and pushes the shoulders away from the head, producing the same stretch as above. It is probably a good idea to start with pushing first one shoulder, then the other, back and forth, gently at first, and then building up pressure.

Holding Points

This is the key technique, if not the only one, of many of the schools of subtle acupressure. Using this technique, the acupressurist does not stimulate the points very much, if at all, through the use of pressure. The points are simply gently touched with the tip of the finger and held in this manner for some time, typically one to three minutes.

While holding the points, the focus of the acupressurist is on the inner energy, using visualization with breath. In this way the acupressurist "channels" energy to and through the person being worked on.

This style of acupressure focuses a great deal on the "feel" of a point and the energy going through it. The acupressurist tries to develop the ability to feel in his or her fingertips the quality of the point, what some call its "pulse." This is not the blood pulse or the pulse felt in the fingertips of the acupressurist. It is the rhythm of the chi flowing through the point when the channel of energy is no longer blocked.

The acupressurist, in this style, relies on the power of the

125

chi alone. It is not necessary, these schools maintain, to facilitate the energy flow through any manipulation of the physical anatomy, such as massage or pressure of some other sort. The rebalancing of the chi occurs only through subtle influence. While schools such as Jin Shin Do and reiki advocate for this approach, it is used in other schools as well. Most acupressurists use this technique at one time or another. It can be a very powerful one.

The strength and effectiveness of this approach rely on a strong and consistent practice on the part of the acupressurist. Some people who practice reiki say that it is a natural event to have the energy transferred from one person to another. This may be so. But the tradition of the Taoist masters concerning this holds that (right) practice is central to the proper and effective use of chi energy in this manner. There are dangers to both people when done otherwise.

The practice of meditation and hara breathing—and regular chi gung and/or t'ai chi—as a path to understanding and controlling chi can prevent a number of pitfalls. These include the depletion of energy in the acupressurist—leading not just to fatigue, but also to real illness; the transfer of energy that is not of a healing sort; and the shifting of energy in the other person which is uncontrolled and too much or too little.

The tradition in China and elsewhere in Asia recognizes the power of the chi energy and respects it. It behooves the acupressurist to take guidance from this tradition, especially as the experience and cultural background in relating to chi are so different.

Given this precaution, the acupressurist should try using subtle acupressure as well as the other forms.

Other Techniques

Other methods specific to the stimulation of points are used, primarily, in medical acupressure, and therefore are more common in China and Japan than in the West. However, you should be aware of them, and you may on occasion find them useful. These methods include:

- Squeezing and pinching of the muscle and ligaments
- Pinching and tweaking of the skin and subcutaneous tissue
- Striking, knocking, and flicking

These techniques are described in many Chinese and Japanese books on masotherapy.

127

.𝒢◡

DOING ACUPRESSURE ON OTHERS

By now you have probably gained a fairly thorough knowledge of your own body and what it feels like, both to your hands and from the inside. But, before you begin to work on yourself or others, you should know what area of the body you are going to work on and why, and you should have a good idea of what to do without referring back to the book.

When using acupressure on another person, you will be faced with a number of choices, among them:

- How should I have the person lie down? Or should the person lie down at all?
- Does the person have to be undressed or can I work with a person who is clothed?

- Where should I put my hands to begin?
- How will I know what to do?
- What should I do first?
- What are the best places to work on the body?
- What is the best way to work on the points?
- What kind of pressure is best?
- How will I know if the acupressure is working?

How to Assess What Is Needed

In Chinese medicine, the practitioner never begins any sort of treatment without a thorough understanding of the dynamics that are contributing to the person's symptoms or discomforts. A diagnosis is made using several well-developed skills of observation. Any of these methods can be applied by an acupressurist, despite the fact that he or she is not attempting to diagnose illness.

These traditional modes of observation are simply the best ones available for getting a good, full picture of a person. To some extent, we all use them in everyday life, even if we do so at an unconscious level. The professional, by becoming conscious of these methods of observation, gains a great deal more information by using them. The methods are:

- Observing the color and demeanor
- Taking the pulses
- Examining the tongue
- Noticing olfactory information (the smell of the person)
- Interviewing

A Chinese acupuncturist in the United States has his desk about thirty-five feet from the entrance to his consulting room. This doctor is able to make an almost complete and accurate diagnosis of his patient by the time the person has walked the distance from the office door to the desk. He confirms his diagnosis by taking the pulses and examining the tongue. His powers of observation and his knowledge of the effects of an imbalance on the color, demeanor, gait, and so forth of the individual are extremely well-developed.

It is unlikely that any of us will ever achieve this degree of sensitivity. But, by being aware of the areas to observe, we can make a fairly good assessment of the general state of a person.

Taking pulses and doing a tongue examination are crucial to diagnosing illness but not to doing acupressure. Some professional acupressurists do both in making their assessments. Some never do either. While the acupressurist may never learn these techniques, he or she should know of their existence and be aware of the Chinese view of the pulses. If a person is interested in pursuing these subjects, they should take a course in them at a school of acupressure or Chinese medicine.

The Chinese have found that there are many pulses. Their location, how to use them, and overall number of pulses are generally agreed upon in the tradition.

Most practitioners use six or twelve pulses. The main pulses are located on the wrist, in the general area where we have become used to feeling for the pulse in the West. However, the Chinese have found three pulse positions on each wrist, with a deep and a superficial pulse in each position. Finding and feeling these pulses takes considerable practice.

129

Pulse Exercise

1. With the palm of one hand toward the chest, place the first three fingers of the other hand under the back of the wrist of the other arm and curved around onto the pulse side of the wrist.

2. The first three fingers are placed together over the bone on the thumb side of the wrist, with the fingertips against the tendon and the first finger just below the wrist fold. You will be able to feel the pulses in each of the three positions. By pressing firmly you will find the three deep pulses.

3. Try feeling for each pulse separately with each finger. By holding your fingers lightly on the surface and pressing very gently, you will find three superficial pulses. Again, use each finger separately. Many people have difficulty finding the third position pulses, so don't worry if you cannot find them.

130

The organ meridians related to each pulse are shown in Table 8.1. Historically, there has been a minor disagreement about which superficial pulses are related to which meridians. You may find some of the pulses listed differently in other books on acupuncture.

The traditional practitioner has many descriptive terms for the quality of the pulses, and the kinds and combinations of the pulses inform as to the imbalances that exist. Pulses can be floating, sinking, slow, rapid, thin, empty, full, slippery, wiry, and so

TABLE 8.1	TABLE OF THE PULSES	

LEFT HAND

Position	Deep	Superficial
First	Heart	Pericardium
Second	Liver	Gall bladder
Third	Kidney	Bladder and large intestine

RIGHT HAND

Position	Deep	Superficial
First	Lungs	Large intestine
Second	Spleen	Stomach
Third	Kidney	Triple warmer and small intestine

forth in a variety of positions and combinations. Even beginning to learn the technique of accurate pulse taking is far beyond most acupressurists. But, exploring can be fun, and you can always get a general impression. For example, a slow pulse can indicate that a person may be getting a damp, cold illness. A rapid pulse indicates heat. These are just two examples, and the combinations render the entire picture more complex.

The observation of facial color, general demeanor, and body posture and gait can give us a great deal of information.

Most of us already instinctively know many ways to "read" the body: we can see exhaustion or sickness in a pale complexion and physical pain or emotional suffering in a drawn, tight appearance. We make these observations almost casually. However, once you begin to pay particular attention, you will learn a great deal about a person from this kind of observation.

One of the major sources of information that you will use is the interview. Generally, you won't sit down and conduct a formal interview. But, you will ask a number of questions, listen to the answers carefully, and verbally explore from time to time as you work with the person and ask for feedback about sore points, tension, stiffness, and so forth.

The verbal interview is crucial to the work of acupressure.

First, the verbal interview can speed the process of learning what it is that you're experiencing with your hands. By asking for feedback, you learn what painful, tense, or tender places feel like. If what you feel as pulse in a point is associated with a reduction of pain, feedback will tell you as much.

Second, and perhaps equally important, the interview is about the only tool that will tell you if there is a serious condition that you must be aware of. This is significant, because you do not want to find yourself doing something that is contraindicated or even dangerous.

Of course, before you even begin an acupressure treatment on someone, you should ask if they have any medical conditions. The conditions to be concerned about include:

- High blood pressure
- Heart disease
- Varicose veins

- Severe skin disease
- Any current illness
- Pregnancy

Choosing a Location

First, select a room that is quiet, private, clean, and nicely decorated. If the weather is nice, you may want to be in a garden area, or on a patio or deck. You will probably want to pick a place that is especially tranquil. You may want a candle burning, or some other source of aromatherapy in the room. (Make sure it is a totally pure, natural oil, not a chemically scented candle.) You may decide to have quiet, meditational music in the background. Be sure and ask the other person if they like it before you play music.

Choose a worktable (massage table or other), a massage chair, or a floor mat that is most comfortable for you. Experiment with as many as different ones as you can. Each has its own fans among professional acupressurists.

133

If you plan only to work on other people once in a while, or just family and friends, a floor pad or mat is an excellent choice. It is also economical. Some professionals work only on the floor because it gives them the ability to move around and over the other person, to shift from massage to shiatsu easily, to work on the person sitting up, and to sit in comfortable proximity to the person being worked on. A single, wide foam mattress or futon works very well. A yoga mat is more portable. You can even place several layers of folded quilts on the floor. Be sure, however, it is very firm while at the same time allowing enough give to be able to slide your hand under a person who is lying down. This is crucial since a great deal of acupressure is done in this manner.

A low table has many of the same advantages as the floor mat, although some acupressurists find it easier to sit next to a low table. The table is always padded or has a thick mat on it, just as if you were working on the floor. It should be very sturdy.

A standard massage table has the advantage of allowing the acupressurist to stand, feel balanced, and walk around easily, and for the person being worked on to lay facedown in comfort because of the face hole. Some stretches you may choose to do are easier on the table, however, and some are not. Some acupressurists like to hold points for long periods of time, and standing in one position while doing this can become tiring. A good massage table will be both sturdy and lightweight, portable, and with adjustable height. They can be reasonably priced or very expensive, depending on their features. Do not buy one without doing extensive research, since they are a considerable investment.

Some acupressurists use a massage-table-high table, which is wider than a standard massage table, has a foam mattress on it, and is great deal more sturdy and can hold more weight. While not portable, this kind of table is economical, since any handyman can make one.

Many people want and need to have their neck, shoulders, and back worked on. A massage chair is admirable for this purpose but restricts work to the upper body and the back, neck, shoulders, and head. In general, it is not a good choice for acupressure, but can be used for specific purposes. These fully adjustable, special chairs tend to be at least as expensive as a massage table, if not more so, and they severely limit the ability to do real acupressure.

Most acupressure is done while the person who is being worked on is fully clothed. If you both are comfortable, you can certainly work on a person who is undressed, as in traditional massage. Some acupressure therapists have the person being worked on remove their shirt and leave shorts or underwear on. That way, the acupressurist can see the skin and musculature as well as feel it. If you choose to work this way, be sure to drape the person with sheets. In either case, be certain to have a couple of lightweight blankets available for warmth. When a person begins to relax, the body temperature will often drop and the person may feel chilly.

Acupressure is done without massage oil. The oil interferes with the quality and feel of the skin and the ability to press on points without slipping. If the person is wearing light clothing, the cloth won't interfere with the ability to press points.

Starting an Acupressure Session

You will probably find that you want to start with the person lying on his or her back. This position effectively promotes relaxation. Some acupressurists who like to do a heavier massage on the back may begin by working with the person on the stomach. However, you will find that you can work on the back very well for most things in the back down position.

If the person is on their stomach, be sure to ask if they need a pillow under their stomach to ease any lower back strain, or under their feet to raise them, for the same reason. If on their back, a pillow under the knees relieves lower back stress.

Begin by observing their breath and by centering and relaxing your own. Take as much time as you need. It will help you both "get in tune."

If the person is on the stomach, stand at their head. Place your hands on the upper back, and just let the person rest there as you feel their breathing. Center yourself in your own breathing. Then try to feel the quality of the person's energy. If you sense tension, do not move your hands, but let them rest a few minutes

135

longer. This slight pressure over the lungs is often very quieting and allows a person to relax.

If you continue to feel tension, or if you simply feel that it's an appropriate move, slide your hands down the back to the waist, exerting moderate pressure, and then let your hands rest again on the upper back.

At this point, you may have some specific work you want to do on the back. It might be deep work on specific points along the bladder meridian. It might be some form of heavy pressing or rubbing. In any case, it would not necessarily be part of opening a treatment session. Whatever it is, after completion you will have the person turn onto their back, stomach up.

With the stomach up, position yourself at the head of the person. Place your hands on the upper part of the chest, above the breast tissue on a woman, and focus on the breathing, as described above. If the person seems excessively tense, place your hands on the upper arms, with the palms cupping the shoulders and the fingers flat but slightly pressing in. This way of holding is very comforting to most people. Just hold this position for two or so minutes.

Now that your hands are cupping the shoulders, you can gently stretch the shoulders away from the head by pressing gently but firmly toward the feet. Push with the weight of your body, not your arm muscles. This is a smooth movement from your own center into the other person's body, shifting energy down. Imagine the other person relaxing down. Push, and release the pressure. You may find that it is easier and more effective to press first on one shoulder, then on the other, back and forth rhythmically. If so, do this several times. Then return your hands to the person's upper chest, as before. This kind of stretching can help relax a person a great deal.

136

Signs of relaxation at this point, or at any time, will often include a deep breath or a sigh. The more relaxed you can help the person to be, the better. It is much easier to find tense areas when there is overall relaxation. When the entire body is slightly tense, it is often difficult to find an area that is tense in relation to the rest of the body.

Next, hold the person's head in your hands, with your fingers under the base of the skull and the head cradled in the palms of your hands. With your fingers firmly curved into the neck, pull the head away from the body. Do this by leaning back and pulling with you entire arms, using the weight of your body. This results in a smooth pull from your own hara and does not produce any strain. This stretch is very good for relaxation. Do not do this stretch if the person has or has had a neck injury.

137

Now go to the person's feet and hold them with the ankles cupped in the palms of your hands. Try doing this with their big toes touching. This seems to help the body energy move down.

At this point you may also wish to do a stretch to each leg, following the instructions already given for stretching.

If you have not already done so, you should ask the person what areas of the body need the most attention, where there is tension, pain, or stiffness. Use your hands to gently explore these areas as the two of you talk. Get verbal feedback to determine the location and extent of any problem. As the person is most likely still lying on his or her stomach, it will be easy to explore areas of the back that may be causing trouble. Remember, at this point you are still getting a feel for what is going on and not trying to do anything other than promoting further relaxation.

From this point on, you will be using the guidelines in the

rest of the book. However, there are some basic guidelines to working on another person.

Ending an Acupressure Session

As you approach the end of an acupressure session, it is very important to leave the person as relaxed as possible and with the energy in a balanced state of harmony. This can be achieved by using a few select points and holding them very quietly for several minutes. This is done in such a way that the person's energy is well-contained in the body, even if they drifted off to sleep, which is often the case.

When you're ready to end, position yourself at the foot of the person and hold the entire toe end of each foot in each of your hands, cupping your fingers over the toes. Bring the feet next to each other so the heels and the big toes are touching. Hold the feet in this position for two or three minutes. If you have ended your treatment by working on the feet, this will be a natural conclusion.

Move and comfortably position yourself at the head of the person.

Place your fingertips gently but firmly on the forehead just above the eyebrow ridge. Let them rest there for one or two minutes. Focus your own breathing on the hara.

Now, remove one hand and gently place it on the upper chest, the entire hand resting palm down, resting firmly but not exerting any more pressure than that of the weight of your hand. Slide the other hand so the fingertips lie on the area of the "third eye." Again, hold these two points for one or two minutes.

138

You will probably now want to shift your position to the side of the person, though if you have long arms, you may be comfortable doing the next points without moving.

Remove the hand that you are using to hold the "third eye" and place it over bai hue, the crown chakra, on the top of the head. Keep your other hand on the upper chest and hold these two points for one or two minutes. If you feel so inclined, you may move the hand from the upper chest and gently place it over the person's hara. Again, hold for one or two minutes. It is very important to keep your own breathing and consciousness centered in your own hara.

This ending pattern is designed to reestablish the energy in a smooth flow along the central channels of the body. If you have become accustomed to using inner imagery as you work, you may use your own consciousness to enhance this effect.

It is advisable to allow the person to lie undisturbed for several minutes following an acupressure treatment. Under ideal circumstances, this amount of time would be extended to a half an hour. Practically, this is rarely possible. But the person should be advised to rest or even take a nap after leaving an acupressure session. This will allow time for the body to readjust to the new flows of energy that have been achieved.

139

BASIC ACUPRESSURE GUIDELINES

The following guidelines are rarely found in books on acupressure. Instead, they are learned through trial and error. However, they certainly bear mentioning.

Learn from Your Hands

Stay focused on the information your hands are giving you. You may have formed some ideas of what you want to do based on your observations and what the person tells you. However, if you stay with this, which really amounts to only using your mind, you will miss the constant flow of information that you would otherwise be experiencing. Very often the hands will be the best source of information. One famous osteopath never made a decision to do any adjustment on a patient until she had "scanned" the person's entire body with her hands.

Determine the
Overall Quality of Chi

Think about the overall primary direction of the flow of chi in the person and its quality.

Is the person exhibiting the qualities of excessive upward flow of chi? These might include headaches, sinus congestion, earaches, being "stuck in their head" (a sort of mental approach to everything), being "ungrounded," and so forth.

Is the overall quality of chi slow, or sluggish? Is the person constipated, overweight, tired, or just sort of slow? Other symptoms might include excess appetite or poor appetite, coldness, a general impression of heaviness.

Think about other similar questions to ask yourself regarding the quality of the chi.

Now think about whether you want to focus on any particular meridian or simply on enhancing the flow of energy in a particular direction. If you choose to help the energy to flow downward, for example, think about the yang meridians and work more on them. If you sense that there is a general need for the person to experience more nurturing in his or her life, think about the yin meridians, and especially the conception vessel.

These are just suggestions. The overall issue is to remember to determine the general quality of the person you are about to work on. You do not want to do highly energetic and energizing work on a person who walks in wound up as tight as a watch spring. On the other hand, this may be just what is needed for a person who is chronically depressed.

Use Imagery and Inner Perception

141

In doing many of the exercises on yourself in this book, you have used your consciousness and inner imagery to enhance and direct the flow of your own chi. It is absolutely essential to continue to follow this practice when working on others.

You will discover that you can aid the movement of the chi in another person with your hands. This is not very difficult. However, controlling this ability and using it with sensitivity to aid another requires that you stay focused, with your consciousness on the appropriate images, and that you intentionally direct the flow of your own breath and energy.

The worst massage I ever had was by a person who talked to the massage therapist at the next table during the entire time she was working on me. Because her awareness was somewhere else, she exhibited no sensitivity, no awareness of whether she might be causing me any pain. She left me, therefore, with more tension than what I had when I came in. This woman claimed to have been trained in acupressure and reflexology.

Do Not Ever Lose Contact
with Your Own Hara

This is the center of the chi energy in your body and the resource for all of the work. Remember, while acupressure often resembles massage on the surface, it is fundamentally work with the body's energy.

Practice hara breathing daily. Do it before and during your practice of acupressure. If you do, you will find that you'll not only help the other person restore balance, but that you will also become more refreshed while doing the work.

9

Finding
Key Points

Every main organ meridian has a specific number of points
on it. These points are the places, long recognized from
centuries of use, where the chi energy of the meridian can be
activated. It is this activation that is used to balance the energy
flow in the body.

There are at least 365 commonly used points recognized
by acupuncturists in TCM. In addition to points on the main
meridians, "extra points" have been clinically shown to have
well-recognized uses. Some of these extra points are on the ear,
for example, and on the feet.

Acupressure uses exactly the same points as acupuncture.
However, most acupressurists in the West use far fewer points
than acupuncturists. There are two reasons for this. First, acupressurists in the West are not treating complex illnesses. Most
acupressure is done for minor aches and pains, for purposes of

general rejuvenation, for balancing and harmonizing the body, and for enhancing health. The second reason is that some of the points simply cannot be used except through needling.

Some systems of acupressure, such as Jin Shin Do, use far fewer points than either acupuncture or traditional Chinese-based acupressure. This is for theoretical reasons only.

As you learn and discover your own capabilities, you will make choices about how many points you want to learn about and how many you will include while working with others. Most acupressurists keep meridian and point charts on the walls of their workrooms for easy reference and a good reference book on point usage available.

The points I've chosen to discuss were selected because of their importance and widespread applications. Both their location and traditional uses will be described. In many instances their function in acupressure has been expanded to include more emotional qualities. In some instances, the Chinese understanding of why a point is used to treat a specific condition will be outlined. This will help explain why a single point might apply to many different situations. For example, using *hoku* to reduce the pain of a headache and to aid in delivery during labor works in both instances, because the general function of the point is to move chi energy downward in the body.

The points specific to an organ meridian are important, as are those on the junction of an organ meridian, which have a strange flow. Key points on the main organ meridians help regulate the energy flow in that meridian, and, sometimes, they have a referring function to another meridian. When the point lies at a junction with a strange flow, it can be used to release a reserve of energy that may be needed or release an excess of energy.

Some of these key points are used because they are known to have a general overall effect on the whole body. These will be described individually.

In thinking about the points and their uses, remember that the meridians are not separate entities, but a network of inter-connected and interrelated channels performing an overall function of balancing the entire organism. The points can then be seen as gateways that regulate the flow.

We have already described, in some detail, the ways in which a point can be found and recognized with the fingers and otherwise. Now, the location of specific points will be delineated and the primary use given. In most instances, their traditional and medical use will be described, even though the approach to acupressure presented here is not specifically a medical one. In addition, other, perhaps more modern, uses will be described.

These points are listed and described in no particular order, other than how commonly they are used. In fact, they are all used quite often. Some are so widely used, even in the West, that they are referred to by their Chinese names.

Points are usually designated by their universally used shorthand name. These consist of the initials of the meridian name—for example, GB for gall bladder—and the number assigned to the point, starting with the beginning point of the meridian. So, for example, GB 1 is the starting point of the gall bladder meridian. You will see this below, though in many cases the meridian is spelled out.

In some cases, the English translation of the Chinese name will be given because, as already mentioned, the imagery of these names can be helpful in experiencing the quality of a point. Of course, while many of the points have imagery attached to them,

145

some of these translated names might not mean much to you because of cultural differences. (In some books from China translated into English, the points may be designated only by their Chinese name. This was certainly not intended to drive a Westerner crazy, but it does, unless you're a student of classical Chinese.)

IMPORTANT POINTS

We will not include many points in this chapter. Most points will only be used in combination with other points in a general, overall treatment pattern for specific conditions. But the points described here can be used alone, and often are.

GV 20: Bai Hui

This point has already been discussed in reference to the hara breathing exercise. (See Chapter 5.) It is the point that in other traditions is the seat of the crown chakra.

The point is located on the centerline of the head, directly above the top of the ears, in a slight depression in the skull.

The traditional uses for this point include treating headaches, dizziness, heaviness in the head, nasal congestion, inability to choose words, forgetfulness, and even mild insanity. However, its real significance lies in the fact that it is the entrance point for universal energy moving in a downward direction into the body. While it is not the last point on the meridian, it is the top of the head and associated with one of the great energy centers of the body. So it can be seen as the top of an energy flow from the lower part of the body, specifically from both GV 1 and from the hara.

Recognizing that this point is key to the energy moving up and down in the body on this inner axis, through the chakras, is crucial. In Chinese medicine and osteopathy, the energy is described as running up and down the spinal column area. But in other traditions—including the Hindu, Tibetan, and Balinese tradition of the chakras—this point is the top of an inner channel of energy through the chakras. The depiction of this energy channel appears in many Tibetan paintings. In these same traditions, this point is also considered the entrance and exit point for spirit.

From this latter point of view, the effectiveness of this point for "insanity" can be seen. People, including children, who have problems staying in their bodies, who tend to drift off a great deal, or who report that they leave their bodies, can be helped to stay physically grounded by using this point. This is achieved by laying one hand over the area of the point and holding the other hand on some other place on the body, such as the hara or the base of the spine.

Holding this point on almost anyone can be very calming. Holding this point is often combined with holding the area of the heart chakra, or the so-called third eye, at the same time. It is an effective way to "ground" someone at the end of an acupressure treatment. That is to say, the energy of the person, which may have become somewhat "loose" during deep relaxation, can be focused back into the body. Some people say they "drift off." This will bring them back.

This point is closely associated with the fontanel on a newborn infant, which has not yet closed. Experience in acupressure suggests you should not put your hand intentionally over this point for some weeks after birth. The free flow of energy at this point should not be disturbed.

ST 16: Chest Window

This is a connecting point between the stomach meridian and one of the so-called strange flows. It is located on an imaginary vertical line through the nipple, on the chest (where the breast tissue on a woman begins), one rib space above the nipple. It will often be sore. Traditionally, this point is used for shortness of breath, emphysema, breast cancer, and problems with the ribs in this area of the chest.

The name suggests its most positive use in acupressure, in addition to its traditional use of aiding in free breathing. Gentle massage or holding of this point will help open and relax the chest area, resulting in the release of melancholy and the acquisition of a brighter spirit. If you are doing work with a person who is working through a great deal of grief or loss, you may find the person releasing these feelings, including sobbing. The important thing, if this happens unexpectedly while working on someone, is to recognize what is happening and verbalize it for the person.

SP 16: Abdomen Sorrow

This is another point connected to a strange flow. It is located just inside the nipple line on the lowest rib. With your fingers, follow the underside of the rib cage, beginning in the center at the sternum, until you come to an indentation in the bone. Press in and up against the bone.

Traditionally, this point is used for problems with internal organs in this area, including the liver. The problems indicated arc not associated with excess heat and energy, but with the absence of energy and coolness.

These points release tension in the abdominal area and the diaphragm, and thus work on them can help to not only relieve such things as hiccuping and side aches, but can aid in digestion. Also, most important, work on these points can boost the immune system.

Gall Badder 21: Shoulder Well

This point lies on the top of the shoulder, halfway between the end of the bone and the base of the neck. It is actually in a division between muscles, which you can feel with your fingertips. It is very often sore. (Lots of people massage this point on themselves or others without realizing that it is a meridian point.) This point was traditionally used to treat the sexual organs and tightness in that area of the body.

It is a key point for a number of reasons. First, it allows the strange flows in the neck to flow freely up and into the head. Second, it is a point that tightens in response to the common stresses of everyday life. This is the physical center of the state of being that in popular slang is called being "uptight."

These points can be massaged very deeply. This will release shoulder and neck tension; relieve tension headache; and reduce emotional tension and feelings of frustration, of being blocked, and irritability.

It is another of the points that moves energy down.

This point should not be worked on vigorously in a woman who is pregnant. It could promote premature labor.

149

Gall Bladder 20

This point is just under the back of the base of the skull, between the two muscle bands, in a little hollow. The pressure to be exerted is up toward the bone of the skull.

The point is traditionally used for headaches, including migraine; all sorts of eye problems; and many kinds of nose problems. In fact, it has a strong effect on eyes, ears, nose, mouth, and the brain. The point can also be used for colds, flu, and insomnia.

The key to understanding the wide application of the use of this point is that it effects two strange flows. Therefore, it can have a beneficial effect on the entire body.

In the course of an acupressure treatment, this point should be held, with the person on their back, for at least two minutes, if not more. You should apply the hold at the head of the person, sliding your hands under the base of the skull. Then, with fingers curved up against the points, pull back toward yourself. The weight of the head will exert enough pressure on your fingers.

This point has a very calming effect on both the body and mind, as well as being one that is beneficial overall.

Bladder 38

This point is on the outer part of the bladder meridian on the back. It is located halfway between the inner edge of the scapula and the spine, at the level of the space between the fourth and fifth ribs, or the space between the fourth and fifth thoracic vertebra.

Traditionally, this point was used to treat serious and

chronic illnesses. One Chinese doctor writes that this point can "cure one hundred diseases."

This point is very useful for releasing tension from the upper back, regulating breathing, and especially building up general body strength when the person is debilitated. It is another of the points that lies at the junction of a strange flow.

Bladder 38 is often activated by the use of moxa to alleviate exhaustion. Older traditions indicate that this point should not be used with moxa on anyone under the age of twenty because it will produce excessive yang chi.

Bladder 54: Entrusting Middle

This point is located on the back of the knee, directly through the leg from the kneecap, between the two tendons.

Not surprisingly, the traditional use of this point is for knee problems, such as inflexibility and pain. But it is also useful for various problems in the abdominal area.

Many acupressurists have found that this point is very good for relieving lower back pain caused by tension in the muscles, and also for hip pain, weakness in the legs, and leg cramps. Since back pain is often related to the condition of the abdominal muscles, this may partially explain the effect of this point.

With the person lying on the back, legs outstretched, slide one hand under one knee and use your curled fingers to exert pressure on the point. The weight of the leg will maintain the pressure easily. The other hand may be placed under any of the lower back points along the spine. Hold the point for several minutes. Do the same thing on the other side.

Bladder 62

The point is located on the outside of the ankle, just below the anklebone. It will probably be quite tender or sore.

This point is traditionally used for headaches and hypertension. It is also used for general pain control. Its position at the junction of a strange flow helps it to balance the yang energy of the body. It can promote sound sleep when there is a problem with insomnia.

As you can see from its uses, this point has a calming effect on a person who is tense or overenergized. With the person lying down, hold the ankles firmly while at the same time use your fingers to exert firm pressure on the points. Hold the pressure for at least two minutes. For pain control, you may have to exert fairly significant pressure with the tip of your finger, or a knuckle. But do not cause pain under any circumstance.

Gall Bladder 31

When the person puts his or her hands to the sides, while standing, the tip of the middle finger lies on this point. It is on the outside of the leg on the centerline. It is generally quite sore to the touch.

Traditionally, this point is used for leg pain, arthritis, lumbago, lower back stiffness, stiffness of the knees, and itching of the body.

The main function of this point is detoxification of the body and emotions. It can be useful with such a mundane thing as a hangover and with more serious states such as having experienced a "toxic" situation in life. Most people find that release of this point results in an increased sense of "clearness" or "lightness."

The point and the general area around it should be massaged gently but firmly, with increasing pressure on the point as it loses its tenderness.

Spleen 4

This point is located on the inside of the foot, in a groove in the arch just back from the big knucklebone at the base of the big toe, where the white and the red flesh meet. It is usually quite sore.

Also connected to a strange flow, this point has been used for cold feet and foot cramps. More important, it is used for a variety of internal conditions where the yin energy is deficient. When stimulated, this point can help rebalance and redistribute the yin chi throughout the body.

153

While this point, as with others, can be held, it is more effective to stimulate it forcefully with your fingertip, even (carefully) with the edge of the fingernail.

Large Intestine 4: Ho Ku

To find this point, press the thumb and first finger, held straight, together. The muscle between the two, on the hand, will bulge out. The point is on the highest place on the bulge. With the hand relaxed, press on the point toward the bone of the hand, not toward the thumb. It is generally sore.

This point has been used for a variety of disorders of the head and face, such as toothache, tonsillitis, stuffed nose, and everything wrong with mouth. It is said to be useful in the case of flu.

The key to understanding the function of this point is that it moves the energy of the body down. It is very powerful. In addition to the above-mentioned uses, it can be helpful for treating headache, sinus congestion, and constipation. In fact, any condition where excess energy needs to move down can be positively affected.

Do not use this point on a pregnant woman.

THE FIVE CONTROLLING POINTS

The following points are said to control the energy in general areas of the body, and they are used when there are any problems in these areas. The points may be held until the pulse is felt, or they may be gently massaged or pressed.

Stomach 36: Entire Abdominal Area

This point is on the outer side of the leg, three finger widths below the knee, on the edge of the shinbone. It is often quite sore.

The usefulness of this point, according to TCM, is extensive. Not only is it used to treat a wide range of stomach, digestive, and gastric disorders, but it has also been used to aid in melancholia, excessive fear and anger, and mania. It has long been known that moxa applied to this point promotes general health and longevity.

Lung 7: For the Head and Neck

The point is located on the inside of the lower arm, on the thumb side, two finger widths from the wrist crease and against the bone, where the red and the white flesh meet.

It is said that this point can help move all of the chi in the entire body. Thus, it treats stagnant conditions such as chest congestion, migraine headaches, melancholy, facial paralysis, stiff neck, and forgetfulness.

Bladder 54: For the Back

See Chapter 11.

Pericardium 6: For the Chest to the Navel

This point is located on the palm side of the wrist, two finger widths from the wrist crease, between the two tendons. It is used for all kinds of stomach problems and problems with the esophagus. It relieves problems of the chest and upper abdomen. In addition, it can help relieve cramping and pain in the arm.

155

Large Intestine 4: (Ho Ku) For the Face and the Mouth

See Chapter 12.

THE YU POINTS

The bladder meridian is the longest meridian on the body. As previously mentioned, it has a double channel on the back parallel with the spine. Along these paths lie what the Chinese call yu points. Some of the bladder meridian points, but not all of them, are yu points. Each of these yu points has a correspondence with one of the major organs or areas of the body. (See Figure 9.1.)

Notice that the points are in the same order from top to bottom as the organs or areas of the body that each is related to. This makes locating the correct yu point relatively easy while doing acupressure on a person.

The function of the yu points is twofold in TCM. The first is diagnosis, and the second is treatment. In acupressure, we can make use of the yu points to evaluate the condition of a person's energy and to focus the acupressure in certain areas and on specific meridians.

The method of working on the back has already been described. In using the yu points to evaluate a person's condition, it is probably easiest to have the person sit up or lie on his or her stomach. This allows you to press the points firmly and to move from point to point easily.

In general, when a yu point is tender or tense to the touch, it is an indication of imbalance in the corresponding organ meridian or body area.

When a yu point has been found that indicates an imbalance, the point itself may be used to restore balance. Holding the point with very firm pressure is usually the best method of rebalancing the energy. Sometimes massage on these points just causes more tension. With practice you will be able to feel the point soften and sense the pulse in it.

Figure 9.1 provides a quick reference, but remember, the points we have described in this chapter are by no means all or even a large portion of the most important points used in acupressure. They are a beginning guide to facilitate you in using acupressure. All of these points are well-known and often used.

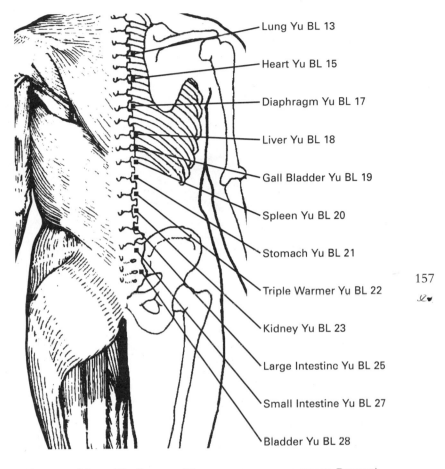

Lung Yu BL 13

Heart Yu BL 15

Diaphragm Yu BL 17

Liver Yu BL 18

Gall Bladder Yu BL 19

Spleen Yu BL 20

Stomach Yu BL 21

Triple Warmer Yu BL 22

Kidney Yu BL 23

Large Intestine Yu BL 25

Small Intestine Yu BL 27

Bladder Yu BL 28

157

FIGURE 9.1.   YU POINTS (ORGAN CORRESPONDENCE POINTS)
OF THE BLADDER MERIDIAN

Other key points in the application of acupressure will be indicated in the chapters on the various conditions. You will also find other useful points indicated in other books. Both books on acupressure and on acupuncture will be helpful.

PART IV

ACUPRESSURE FOR SPECIFIC CONDITIONS

10

Acupressure
for Relaxation and
Rejuvenation

This is the first of several chapters that deals with specific uses of acupressure and the common complaints of people coming to an acupressurist. You will find suggestions for the use of specific points on meridians, and the method and sequence for using them. The location of the points will be described in detail, but in understandable language. To see the location of the energy channels being referred to, consult the meridian charts in the back of the book.

While the approach to this point has been on using your hands to inform yourself of the areas of the body and the points on the meridians needing attention, in this and succeeding chapters we will take the more traditional approach of using designated points.

In acupressure you do not have to learn the exact location of the points with the precision of those who use needles.

Massage or pressure exerted in the general area of the point is often enough to be effective. But you will have to learn the location of some of the key points. It is not possible to do effective acupressure otherwise. Note, however, that what we discussed to this point is still valid. You should trust your own hands and sensitivity. In this way, you will expand your approach and not fall into the trap of just doing someone else's treatment plan by rote.

REVIEWING THE MERIDIANS

Before beginning to examine acupressure for particular conditions in this chapter and those to follow, you should review the description of the main meridians earlier in the book. Refresh your memory as to the general function of energy represented by each meridian. This is enormously valuable in helping you understand why certain specific points may be used.

It's also important to review so you can begin to think in terms of the big picture—of the whole body. You should have this context when focusing on specific points.

It is quite easy to get lost in the details of the points. Yes, the points are important and their uses well-known. But the acupressure points are only *activation points* for the entire meridian. And if you have the function of the meridian in mind, you will be able to work on a person without having to know exactly where the point is.

Always remember that a great deal of shiatsu is based on using pressure over large areas of the surface of the body, and not, as in Chinese Tui Na, using tiny focused pinches, tweaks, and presses on exact points, as useful as they are.

Use the imagery of a meridian's function to give you the sense of what can be accomplished by working on that particular area.

For example, take the spleen meridian. It is said that the spleen chi grasps the blood. What does this image tell you about the possible uses of working on the spleen meridian? Among other things, it suggests that the meridian is related to female blood cycles; to the possibility of anemia and the problems associated with it, such as weakness, paleness, poor metabolism, and general coldness or chilliness; to loss of blood through hemorrhaging. In all of these instances, work on the spleen meridian will be helpful.

This is not to say that the use of specific points is not important. It is. But the overall function of the meridian is just as important. That is one reason why the exercises that focus on strengthening the overall meridian are so useful in promoting and maintaining health.

163

RELIEVING FATIGUE

Acupressure has some specific approaches to promoting general relaxation, or to help overcome tiredness and fatigue. In these cases, the goal is to promote the rebalancing of the flow of chi in the meridians and to restore the body's capacity to heal and energize itself.

In fact, recovery from tiredness and fatigue is one of the most common uses of acupressure. Even if you choose to work on a specific problem area, bringing about a state of relaxation will most likely be a part of every treatment. For many acupressurists, it may be the only kind of treatment that they do.

By learning the basics of how to help the body rejuvenate and become more energized, you will acquire the techniques needed to work on specific problems and areas. As with all the other aspects of acupressure, you must do hands-on practice to truly assimilate the lessons. Try each of the following techniques on yourself or a good friend. You may want to include some of the techniques of Western massage such as the use of massage oil and the long, deep strokes of Swedish style massage.

In any case, use the techniques on various parts of the body and do them many times. This will give you feel for the amount of pressure that can be comfortably applied and the types of pressure that can be used on each part of the body.

164

A variety of specific symptoms can signal that tension is accumulating in the body and that general relaxation or rejuvenation is called for. We should always remember that chronic tension and the failure to relax can lead to far more severe problems than just sore shoulders. Extreme conditions such as chronic headaches, high blood pressure, heart palpitations, and even stroke or heart attack can result from unrelieved chronic tension.

Neither acupressure massage nor Western massage should ever be done on a person who is extremely debilitated, who suffers from chronic fatigue, has heart disease, has a serious skin disease over most or all of the body, or who otherwise is seriously ill. Also, specific precautions should be taken if the person has varicose veins in the legs or is pregnant.

There is a style of subtle acupressure that can be used in these cases, provided the person has received permission from his or her health care provider, and the acupressurist feels sufficiently familiar with the problems to proceed.

On Beginning

When doing acupressure for relaxation and rejuvenation, you will probably want to work on a mat or table rather than a massage chair. The prone body position is most conducive to full relaxation, and it renders all parts of the person's body easily accessible. Now you are ready to begin.

The general guidelines for what to do next have already been presented in Chapter 8. The sequences suggested will ensure that the person on whom you are working is relaxed and receptive to further work. By using the same opening sequence with everyone, you will become increasingly confident of your ability to do effective acupressure.

The sequences, which can be used singly or together, are designed to promote relaxation and general well-being, though they use recognized meridian points and may have other benefits. Further, they can be used when there are no specific complaints, as when a person wishes to regain a sense of well-being, and they may also be used to support overall health.

RELEASING THE BREATH

Near the beginning of an acupressure treatment, it is a good idea to help the person you are working on deepen his or her breath and open up the central channel of energy. This will relax him or her and encourage the energy from the hara to flow upward.

Place one hand under the person's back and find the area about an inch below the bottom of the scapula and an inch out from the spine. Curve all of your fingers up into this area so the point(s) are being firmly pressed.

165

With your other hand, exert gentle but firm pressure on the point just below the rib cage, on the nipple line. The point is against the bone and may be tender, so move into the point slowly. Encourage the person to take several deep breaths, slowly, exhaling through the mouth. Tell the person to let the abdomen expand as he or she inhales.

Do this on both sides.

RELEASING THE LOWER BACK

One way to release the back, which is comforting to most people, is to rock the lower body while holding points on the lower back.

While lying on his or her back, have the person raise one knee. Position yourself on that side and put your hand—the one closest to his or her head—under the lower back. With your fingers, find the meridian along the spinal column. Slide your fingers down until they are on the sacral bone, and, with your fingers curved, let the weight of the person's body exert pressure on the points on the sacrum.

Place your other arm under the person's raised knee, so you can hold the weight of the leg. Have him or her relax and let you support the leg. Now, gently rock the leg from side to side, so the knee swings in an arc, the foot resting on the table. Do not force the extent of the stretch.

Do this again, after moving your hand, which is under the back, up the spinal column a few inches. Rock the leg again several times. In this way you will be releasing the bladder meridian points up the lower back.

Do this on both sides.

RELAXING THE LEGS AND FEET

Begin by doing several stretches on both legs. Then gently rotate the feet at the ankles to help further relax the legs. If you feel comfortable doing so, have the person raise both knees so the legs are bent and the feet flat on the table or mat. Place one of your arms under the bent knees, holding them together and supporting their weight, and gently rock the knees from side to side. This helps relax the hip joints, which further relaxes the legs.

Now massage the meridians on the legs. Use pressure from the thumbs or palms. Gently but firmly, squeeze or press all along the legs on the meridian lines.

Massage and press the area around the anklebones on both sides of the ankles.

Finally, firmly press the entire area of the pad of the heal on each foot.

TONIFYING THE INNER ORGANS

The methods presented here are taken from TCM, osteopathy, and reflexology. They are easy to use and very effective.

One method is to massage the bottom of the feet. If you have just completed the leg relaxation sequence above, this is a natural continuation.

Use your thumbs to press the entire bottom of first one foot and then the other. Every point on the bottom of the foot should be pressed firmly and deeply. This takes time. You will only be moving your thumb from area to area a quarter of an inch at a time. If you consult a foot reflexology chart, you'll find that

167

every area of the bottom of the foot corresponds to an inner organ of the body. However, it is not necessary to know what area corresponds to what inner organ in order to do this foot massage. By pressing these points, you help tonify the entire body system.

A second method is to massage a series of key points. Begin with the points on the central channel on the top of the head, followed by massaging the points at the top of the neck along the base of the skull. Take your time. These points, especially at the base of the skull, take time to open. In this way the point GV 2 (Bai Hui) is stimulated, as well as the key points BL 10 and GB 20. Follow this by a massage of all of the yu points on the back. (See the chart of yu points in Chapter 9.)

RELAXING THE ARMS AND HANDS

Begin with the person on his or her back.

Using the technique for stretching already described, stretch each arm and swing the straight arm in the shoulder socket, as if the person were flying with his or her arms. Do not overstretch or move the arm too quickly or too far. Respect the natural motion and limits of the body. Lay the person's arm back down in a natural position.

Gently massage all the meridian lines on the arm by squeezing with your thumbs or using the palm of your hand to exert firm pressure.

With your fingers, massage all the points in the hollows around the elbow joint and then the wrist.

End by using your thumb to press and massage the pad of the hand at the base of the thumb. Then gently squeeze each finger on the top and bottom (not the sides) between your thumb and forefinger, moving along the fingers to the tips.

RELEASING THE UPPER BACK AND SHOULDERS

With the person on his or her back, position yourself at his or her head and cup the shoulders in your hands. Use your own weight to press each shoulder, one at a time, toward the person's feet. Do not bend your arms, but rather, use your body weight to provide the pressure. Rock back and forth, pushing first one shoulder and then the other.

Now apply pressure on the points along the base of the skull. Use your curved fingertips to do this. The points are against the bone. Do this slowly and firmly. Take your time and hold the points for a couple of minutes.

Now massage the points that are located on the top of the shoulder, halfway between the neck and the tip of the shoulder. Use your thumbs and your body weight to apply deep pressure. Because these points are often very sore and the area around them very tense, use the pressure-release technique to help the muscles relax and the points to release.

Slide your hands under the person's shoulders and find the depression in the center of the scapula. Curve your fingers into this point and let them rest there for a minute or two. Then slide them down to just below the bottom tip of the scapula and curve them into this point. Again, let them rest there, with the weight providing the pressure.

169

BALANCING AND
PROMOTING HARMONY

Post yourself at the side of the person and place one hand gently on the area above the bottom of the breastbone. Place the other hand over the hara. Hold these two areas for a minute or two. Then move the hand that was on the lower chest to the crown of the head. Gently hold these two points for a minute or two.

Finally, place one hand under the base of the skull at the top of the spine and the other at the base of the spine under the tip of the tailbone. Hold these two areas for two or three minutes while focusing on hara breathing.

11

Acupressure
for Muscle and
Joint Problems

M any of the most common complaints center on stiffness, soreness, or pain in muscles, joints, and areas of the body that rely on these, such as the back, shoulders, arms, hands, and knees. Acupressure has not only been used successfully in helping people with these problems, but often it may be one of the few approaches that can be used. For example, acupressure is enormously effective in relieving the pain of simple arthritis where other approaches have failed. And using specific points can often help relieve lower back pain without resorting to pain killers or medical interventions.

The complaints addressed in this chapter might well fall within the category of medical problems. I've already noted the precautions necessary when a serious medical problem might exist, and I will do so again. It cannot be stressed enough: it is extremely important that a medical–type complaint should be evaluated by a health practitioner. These include conditions such as a fractured bone, torn ligaments, or a crushed spinal disk.

This is not to daunt you about the efficacy of acupressure, which can give great relief to the body's pains and aches. Even the pain of a serious back problem can be relieved with the use of subtle acupressure, which cannot further injure the back because it does not use significant pressure.

LUMBAR STRAIN AND PAIN

Back pain is one of the most common complaints. Severe lower back pain should be taken as an indication of a severe back problem, and the acupressurist should send the person to an experienced physician. The causes of back pain can range from actual injury to referred pain from internal organs such as the kidneys or from uterine cramps in women. Even experienced physicians can have difficulty in diagnosing the cause of back pain. Be absolutely certain that you do not do any kind of massage on a back that might cause further injury, should one be present.

Given this warning, relief from mild lower back pain is achievable with acupressure. One should also be aware that sometimes a diagnosis of a slipped disk can be a catchall term for unexplained back pain caused by such things as weak musculature, excess body weight, poor posture, or tension. But if the pain is severe, assume there really is a severe problem.

With the person lying on his or her back, use the tips of the fingers to apply pressure to both the inner and outer bladder meridian points below the rib cage down to the end of the coccyx or tailbone. Start on the outer bladder meridian first, just below the rib cage on one side. Hold the points until you feel them soften and relax. Move your hands down, on the same line, and hold the next series of points. Do this until your lower hand has covered the points to the end of the coccyx. Releasing the points on the outer meridian line first usually facilitates the release of the points on the inner meridian line.

Begin again just below the rib cage, on the inner bladder meridian line. These are the points right along the vertebra. Again, hold the points until you can feel them soften or the muscles relax or when you can feel a pulse.

You do not have to worry about using the correct points because you will actually be holding them all with this technique.

Now, firmly massage the point GB 29, which is located on the side of the hip about one inch above the widest point of the hipbone. The point is just to the rear of the bone and will be quite painful. If you do not think you can locate the point in this way, use your thumbs to massage the area. Do both sides.

Massage SP 9, on the outer side of the leg immediately below the large bone that sticks out just below the knee at the shin. The point is in a hollow.

Massage ST 36, on the outer side of the calf about three finger widths below the knee on the outer edge of the shinbone.

Massage SP 6, on the inside of the lower leg on the shinbone, three finger widths above the anklebone.

Finally, hold the point BL 54 directly behind the kneecap, between the two tendons, with the tip of one finger, allowing the leg to exert pressure. Hold for at least two minutes.

GENERAL BACK PAIN AND TENSION

With the person is on his or her back, work on one side completely, then the other. Place the fingers of one hand on BL 54, directly behind the kneecap. Let the weight of the leg exert pressure on the tips of the fingers.

With the other hand, massage first BL 67 on the outside of the little toe, at the corner of the nail. Then massage BL 62 on the outside of the ankle just below the anklebone.

Now switch hands so your other hand is under the knee, freeing one hand to work on the arm and torso. Keep pressure on BL 54.

Massage TW 5 on the back of the wrist, in the center about two finger widths above the crease line, between the two bones.

With the same hand, hold the points along the outer bladder meridian, starting at the hip and moving up, as follows:

1. BL 48, the point in the hollow of the hipbone, in the buttock. Use all of the fingers together to exert pressure. This point may be very tender. Hold until you feel a pulse or you sense relaxation of the area.
2. Move the hand that is behind the knee to this point and hold it while you continue to work on the rest of the points up the torso.
3. BL 47, on the outer bladder meridian, the point halfway between the rib cage and the top of the hipbone, on the muscular band parallel to the spine.
4. BL 42, on the outer bladder meridian, on a horizontal line from the spine about two finger widths below the tip of the scapula, on the muscle band.

5. BL 38, between the fourth and fifth rib on the outer bladder meridian. It often feels like a knot and is quite tender.

6. TW 15 on the top of the upper tip of the scapula.

7. An extra point on the neck, halfway between the shoulder and the base of the skull, on the outside of the spine. This point can be massaged with the fingers to good advantage.

8. Finally, GB 20 at the base of the skull in a hollow between muscle bands. Hold this point with your fingers curled up into the base of the skull.

175

STIFF NECK

This condition often occurs as a result of sleeping in an unusual position, combined with a cold, which causes the muscles to tense up. Other causes include tension or sitting with the head turned in an unaccustomed position for a period of time.

With the person on his or her back, gently stretch the neck. Follow this with pressing with the thumbs on GB 21, the points on the top of the shoulders, halfway between the base of the neck and the end of the shoulder. The person will tell you when you are on the point, since it will be very tense and sore. Press this point very firmly, using your body weight and not your arms to exert the pressure.

Apply firm pressure to all of the points along the top of the breastbone, starting at the center (CV 22) in the little hollow, and moving toward the shoulders. Press gently at first, because these points can be very tender. Press points on both sides.

Now gently apply pressure to the points on the underside of the jawbone, toward the back. You can feel where the bone at the rear of the jaw turns up. Start applying pressure on the points before the jaw goes up, and then carefully move your fingers back and up along the bone. Press against the bone, not into the soft tissue of the throat. In this way you can apply pressure to the points all the way up and under the ears.

Now, with your thumbs, continue pressing the points behind the ears, on the base of the skull at the joining of the neck. With your fingers curled up, place them under the base of the skull with your forefingers next to the centerline of the neck. Hold the points against the bone, letting the weight of the head apply the pressure. Apply pressure for at least two minutes.

176

STIFF AND SORE SHOULDERS

With the person sitting or on his or her back, gently massage the area on the chest that lies in the hollow between the rib cage, shoulder, and underside of the clavicle bone (above the rib cage at the top of the chest). These points, LU 1 and LU 2, are likely to be very tender.

Now have the person lie on the stomach. If the shoulders are very stiff, a hot towel may be placed across them to aid in relaxation. If this is done, massage the following areas while the towel warms the shoulders:

1. Apply firm finger pressure to the backside of the lower arm from the wrist up to the elbow. Do this gently, giving special attention to the points in the groove between the two bones. At the elbow, press all

the points around the outside of the elbow bone in the various hollows that you can feel.

2. With the elbow bent, find the large hollow on the outside of the upper arm just at the elbow joint. The tips of your fingers will be on the bone of the upper arm. Apply pressure to the points all the way up this bone to the shoulder. Your fingers should be pressing between the two muscles on the upper arm, against the bone. Do both sides.

3. Remove the towels, and use very firm pressure to stimulate the points that lie as follows: in the depression in the middle of the shoulder blade (SI 11); on the inner edge of the shoulder blade halfway between the top and bottom of the bone; and then all of the points that lie on the upper side of the shoulder blade, on the back top of the shoulder, between the neck and the tip of the shoulder.

4. Finally, massage the muscle bands of the neck with downward strokes from the base of the skull. Most acupressurists find that moving the thumbs in a circular motion are best for this.

177

WRITER'S CRAMP
AND SORE WRISTS

These conditions are rarely serious unless there has been an injury.

There are many points on the wrists, arms, shoulders, and neck that can be used to alleviate these problems. Massage paying particular attention to specific areas.

First, press the fingers on the front- and backsides, from the tips of the fingers to the palm of the hand. Then continue pressing points on the palm and the back of the hand in line with the fingers, moving toward the wrist.

Put pressure on all of the points in the wrist area, paying attention to which ones are particularly sore. Remember that the points are in the hollows, within the joints, ligaments, and tendons and between the bones and muscles. You will find them easily. Be careful to put pressure on the large veins on the inside of the wrist. Pressure on all of these points is best accomplished with the pad of the thumb.

Now massage the points in the hollows around the elbow joints.

Massage the points across the top of the shoulder and up the neck to the base of the spine. Again, thumb pressure is probably the easiest way to do this.

Using the palm of your hand, apply a firm rubbing massage to the meridians of the inner arm from the wrist to the elbow to the shoulder, in that direction.

Finally, massage the center of the two pads on the palm of the hand closest to the wrist, using your thumb to press firmly with four fingers on the back side of the hand, squeezing.

SORE ARM MUSCLES

Begin by sliding one hand under the scapula (wing bone) of one side and find the center. Curve your fingers into this point and hold it. Allow the person's body weight to exert the pressure. With the other hand, find the point on the outer arm on the upper part, which is between the split in the muscle at the shoulder (deltoid muscle). Pressing against the bone will generally elicit a pain response because of the tenderness of this point. Use this response to correctly locate this point, but be very gentle. Press and hold the point for thirty seconds or so, release, and press again. Increase the pressure each time. When you feel the point soften and the person reports reduced sensitivity, move to the other side and repeat.

Now press all of the points around the elbow, in the spaces between the bones, in the joint. Follow this with pressing and holding the points across the back of the wrist at the joint, on the crease line. Again, do this on both sides.

End this work on the arms with an arm stretch, as previously described. Leave the arms in a comfortable position.

179

SORE LEG MUSCLES

There are two major contributors to soreness in the legs. One is overuse from exercise. The other is sitting or standing in the same position for a long period of time.

Begin by applying pressure to the points along the outer edge of the spine in the lower back (points on the bladder meridian). You can do this with the person lying on either front or back. If the person is lying on his or her stomach, you may also want to massage the buttocks, using very firm pressure with the palms of your hands. End with the person on his or her back.

If you feel comfortable doing upper leg stretches and rotations, do so. One leg at a time, raise the leg at the knee, instructing the person to relax and let you move the leg. Gently swing the knee from side to side, rotating the leg in the hip joint. Lay the person's leg down, and from the lower leg do a pull stretch. This stretching will aid in the relaxation of the muscles of the leg, so the pressure on the points will be more effective.

Slide one hand under the buttock on one side and use all of the fingers, curled up together, to place pressure in the soft hollow place in the center of the buttock. With your other hand, hold the point on the center of the back of the knee (BL 54) between the two tendons, behind the kneecap. Hold these points for one or two minutes. Do this on both sides.

Now massage the points on the top front of the knee, around the kneecap, and against the bone. Follow this by firmly massaging the point on the outside front of the leg three finger widths below the knee, against the shinbone (ST 36).

Follow this by pressing all of the points down the centerline of the back of the lower leg, starting at the knee. The pressure should be firmly into the musculature, essentially between the two bones, although it will probably feel as if you are against the bone.

Around the ankle area there are many important points. You will find them if you press all around the anklebones on both the inside and outside of the ankle, as well as the center top of the foot where it joins the leg (ST 41).

Finally, massage the points on the bottom of the feet in the center of the arch behind the pad of the big toe (KI 1).

ARTHRITIS AND RHEUMATISM

There are many contributors to the problem of arthritis. From the Chinese perspective, there are four causes of arthritis, and most people in the West would recognize their descriptions. They are arthritis caused by wind, heat, cold, or damp. These four causes can also be in combination. What we in the West identify as rheumatism is cold-damp arthritis, characterized by swelling and pain in response to changes to severe weather. What the Chinese call heat-damp arthritis is close to the serious condition of rheumatoid arthritis.

Acupressure is not a cure for arthritis, and it should not replace consultation with a physician or other health care provider. And it should be recognized that many factors, such as diet, can contribute to the severity of or relief from arthritis.

Given all of this, acupressure can be effectively used for relief of pain and for increased mobility when arthritis leads to a tendency to not move because of the discomfort. The full range of the application of acupressure for relief from arthritis is far beyond the scope of this book. (See the Bibliography for other references). Here, a few main points which have proved helpful are described for your use. In addition to the use of points, a full regimen of exercise is essential. The points are primarily used for pain relief.

The first point to use is LI 1, hoku, on the web of the back of the hand. It is located at the highest point of the muscle when the thumb and forefinger are held close together. When the fingers are spread out, the point is against the bone of the hand, not the thumb.

This point has many applications. It is used here because of its ability to relieve pain because of its anti-inflammatory effect on the body.

LI 10 and LI 11 are located on top of the lower arm on the thumb side. If you bend your arm with your hand flat on a surface, the muscle will bulge at the elbow crease. LI 11 is on the highest part of the muscle. LI 10 is an inch farther toward the

181

wrist, on the meridian. These two points are excellent for pain relief from arthritis in the upper part of the body. The other traditional use is for relief from melancholy (which sometimes takes over a person with arthritis).

GB 34 is located on the outside of the lower leg, about four finger widths below the knee in the space between the two bones. It relieves pain throughout the body, but especially in the legs and knees. It requires firm pressure. Some people use the knuckle of the finger to massage it. It also relieves fatigue and energizes the body.

When the fingers of the hands are very stiff from arthritis, it useful to stimulate the meridians in the fingers as follows:

With the fingers spread apart but relaxed, gently brush the sides of each finger ten times. Start by holding the sides of the thumb at its base and lightly and quickly brush toward the tip. Repeat ten times. Then move to the first finger and repeat this light brushing motion ten times. Do each finger on both hands. This is very soothing, relaxing, and helpful for relief from arthritic stiffness and pain. It can be repeated as often as needed.

12

Acupressure for Common Complaints

At some time or another everyone has complaints about minor illnesses such as a stuffy nose or a headache. Specific acupressure approaches help relieve some of these common complaints and symptoms.

Of course, we should always be aware of the possibility that complaints about what sound like common ailments might be the signals of serious illness. Some people who come to an acupressurist may not recognize the severity of their own symptoms or the implications of symptoms that are only causing them moderate discomfort. For example, upon questioning, a woman who complained of dizziness in the morning revealed that she had been losing weight and had little appetite. The red flag went up for the acupressurist because simple dizziness is not usually related to weight loss. Upon medical diagnosis, it was found that the woman had a serious metabolic disorder.

Medical acupressure should be practiced only by a highly trained person who is appropriately licensed. If there is any question in your mind that the complaint might indicate a medical condition, you should advise the person to seek help from a licensed health care provider.

Some people will seek help from alternative practitioners, including acupressurists, because they do not want to use the services of regular Western medicine. They might have serious medical conditions such as high blood pressure and hypertension, or ulcers or migraines, for example. Employ your best judgment when using acupressure in this situation. You may decide that their choice is an informed one and that you feel comfortable in doing acupressure. But do consider the following:

- Have they been seen by and diagnosed by a physician?
- Do they seem aware of the possible results of not using regular medical forms of treatment?
- Do they believe that you can "treat" them? Are they under the impression that you have a medical skill?
- Do you know the physical effects of the form of acupressure that you choose to use?

Remember these guidelines:

1. Never give a diagnosis of, or a treatment for, an illness or medical condition. Do not give the impression that you are doing this. If you suspect that a serious medical condition exists, insist that the person seek appropriate medical care. Asking an individual about symptoms is not providing a diagnosis; it is an assessment of their condition. Formulating a conclusion that a person has

or doesn't have an illness is a diagnosis. Suggesting that certain symptoms can be relieved with acupressure is not offering treatment. Suggesting that acupressure can cure illness is offering treatment.

2. Always find out if a person has a medical condition, and what they are doing about it if they do have one, before doing acupressure.

3. Do not do any acupressure if you do not understand the nature of a condition that a person has, or if the person has a condition he or she cannot explain to you.

4. Be sure you know if a woman is pregnant. The use of certain points is forbidden in pregnancy, since it could contribute to a spontaneous abortion. (All such specific points mentioned in this book will be identified as such.)

185

Given these precautions, you can comfortably pursue offering relief from the minor symptoms of common complaints through the use of acupressure. What follows are specific acupressure techniques and areas and points to use for problems and conditions. For each one, self-help techniques will be presented first. These will be followed by additional approaches to be used if you are working on another person.

EYE TENSION

Many people suffer from tension in the area of the eyes. This can come from excessive use of the eyes in fine, detail work; long hours of reading or using a computer; hours of driving; and from many other stresses of modern life. Worry, for example, can lead to knitting of the brows, squinting, and so forth, which results in excess tension in the area of the eyes.

The symptoms of eye tension can include squinting, a feeling of tired eyes or of soreness behind the eyes, blurred vision, occasional nearsightedness (those not due to refractive lens problems), dizziness, and watery eyes. Sometimes a frontal headache can be caused by tired eyes and tension in the muscles around the eyes.

Self-Treatment

Lie on your back in a comfortable, relaxed manner. Let your breathing relax and deepen. Rub your hands together to generate heat and chi. Gently place your cupped hands over both of your eyes. Let them rest there a few minutes and continue the relaxed, deep breathing.

Place your thumbs in each eye socket by the bridge of the nose, pressing toward the nose. Press firmly and gently. If the point is sore, press it just until it hurts, holding for perhaps several seconds, and then release. This point is Bladder 1 (Eye Bright) and is useful in a number of conditions related to the eyes. Do this several times until the soreness is reduced or disappears.

Continue using your thumbs to press all of the points in turn around the top of the eye socket, moving them a little a time toward the outside of the eye and pressing upward against the bone. Do not exert pressure against the eyeball itself. Your thumbs should be above the eyeball, pointing upward and pressing up on the bone of the eyebrow ridge.

Now, with your two index fingers, press the points under your eyes by starting at the inside corner of each eye and gently pressing down on the bone. As before, if the points are sore, press the point just until it hurts, hold, and then release the pressure. Do this several times, until the points seem less tender.

Then using all of your fingers together, press gently against the bone above your eye, as before, and slide them outward from the inside corner to the outside corner of the eye. Do this a few times.

Place your fingers above the eyebrows and perform the same outward pressure stroke that you did before, around the eye sockets. You can exert more force with your fingertips in this area. You want to give the tiny muscles in this area a good massage. Give special attention to the point at the outside tips of the eyebrow in the indentation. This is Triple Warmer 23 (Silk Bamboo Hollow) and is specific for eyestrain and pain.

187

Place the index finger of each hand above the top of the eyebrow ridge, directly above the center of the eyebrow and the pupil of the eye. By pressing very firmly, you should feel a small indentation in the bone. This point is Gall Bladder 14 (Yang White) and is a key point for improving night vision; reducing red and swollen eyes; and generally alleviating any problem related to eyestrain, such as frontal headache. Press firmly but carefully on this point. It may be quite sore. Hold for up to two minutes, until you can feel a release.

Now place the fingers of both hands on the area of the face below the temples and in front of the center of the ear, just above the indentation at the jawbone joint. Massage this entire area with firm pressure, using a circular motion with your fingertips.

Place your thumbs on the points at the base of the skull that are just on the outside of the two large muscles that run up the back of the neck. Your hands will cradle the back of your head. This point, Bladder 10 (Pillar of Heaven), is very useful in reducing general tension in the entire head and neck region, getting rid of headache and a general sense of heaviness in the head and the eyes. Massage this point firmly and for at least one minute with your thumbs.

Treating Others

Have the person lie on his or her stomach. Using your thumbs, press the point on top of the shoulder, halfway between the back of the neck and the tip of the shoulder. You should have your thumbs in the indentation between the two muscles that run across the top of the shoulder, pressing down toward the chest. You can do this on yourself by reaching with one hand across your chest and, with your fingertips, finding the point on the opposite shoulder. The point will be very sore because it is a key point for releasing tension in the shoulders and relieving headache. The point is Gall Bladder 21 (Shoulder Well). Massage this point very well. Now massage the entire area from the neck to the ends of the shoulders.

Do not use the point Gall Bladder 21 if the woman is pregnant. This point moves energy in the body downward and is also used to ease difficult labor.

With your thumbs, massage all of the area on each side of the spinal column, moving progressively down the spine until you reach the bottom of the rib cage. This will stimulate many of the key points on the bladder meridian and promote a general balancing of the energy of the body.

SINUS CONGESTION

Sinus congestion and blockage can be caused by a number of things, including allergy and the common cold. If the stuffiness is an acute, temporary condition and known not to be caused by a serious condition, acupressure can give almost immediate relief. Since sinus congestion can cause headache, insomnia, fatigue, and mouth breathing, it should be dealt with quickly.

There is a principle in TCM that points that are far from the problem area are often the indicated points for rebalancing the energy. Alleviating sinus congestion is a good example.

Start by placing your thumbs at the base of the back of the skull, on the hairline, on the outside of the two big muscles that run up the neck, in the depressions. Your hands will be cupping your head over your ears. Under pressure, these points will most likely be quite sore. Press them firmly with the thumbs and massage, and hold them for as long as two minutes. These points will relieve nasal and sinus congestion and a cough that may be caused by sinus problems.

Move your thumbs closer, on the same horizontal line, to the spine, onto the top of the large muscles. Again massage and press these points for a minute or two.

There are a number of points on the head (Bladder 4, Bladder 7, Governing Vessel 21, and Governing Vessel 20—bai wei) that will help. You can massage these points as follows: GV 20 is on the centerline of the head directly between the tips of the ears. Massage this entire area of the head by pressing with your fingertips. The key points will be in the slightly depressed channels of the skull running parallel to the centerline.

If you find that the sinuses above the eyes feel congested or you have a headache in the front of the head or under the forehead, place the right index finger on top of the left eyebrow. Now place the thumb gently in the corner of the right eye against the bridge of the nose. Press the tip of your thumb against the bone, toward your index finger. Gently rotate your thumb slightly until you feel the sore point. Press this point, Bladder 1 (Eye Bright), and gently massage it for a couple of minutes. Do the same to the same point on the other side, using your other hand.

INSOMNIA

190

The person who cannot sleep on occasion, despite a conducive environment and proper diet, can be helped with acupressure. Check his or her back. It is very likely that there will be a stiff area down the neck and back on either side of the spine.

Massage the back of the neck. Then apply pressure to the inner bladder meridian using your fingers, especially to BL 17 on either side of the spine at a level even with the bottom of the shoulder blade; BL 18, two finger widths below that; and BL 23, on the same vertical line, halfway between the bottom of the rib cage and the top of the hipbone. Hold each point for one to two minutes, applying firm pressure.

On the upper abdomen, gently massage the points along the bottom of the rib cage, starting at the centerline and moving outward. Use your thumbs to press in and up against the rib. In this way you will apply pressure to CV 15, ST 19, LV 14, and LV 13.

Finally, suggest that when the person goes to bed, he or she spend a few minutes before falling asleep lying down and placing one hand over the hara and one hand over the center of the chest (the heart chakra). Most people find this very calming and relaxing. Some people who never sleep in this position fall asleep doing this.

HANGOVER

When someone drinks too much at night, it's not uncommon that he or she will feel lousy the next morning. The typical hangover symptoms are headache, nausea, and a general oversensitivity and debility. If this is your condition, try to do the following before rising.

191

Massage the point at the top of head on a line straight upward from the tips of the ears. This is GV 20, Bai Hui. Then massage all along the neck from the spine to under the ears, following the line of the skull. Press the points up against the bone.

Next, massage all of the points along the lower edge of the rib cage on the upper part of the abdomen. Start in the center and move your thumbs outward.

Massage the points between the tip of the sternum down the central line to the navel. Use a firm downward stroke.

Finally, with very firm pressure, using all of your fingers, apply pressure to the points on either side of the navel. By placing your thumbs on the navel, your fingers will be the correct distance out to hold the points. Hold these points for four to six minutes to relieve nausea.

CONSTIPATION

Simple constipation hits everyone at some time or another. If this is not a chronic problem, acupressure can help.

If you wish to help yourself, you can use the point hoku, located on the back of the hand, on the web between the thumb and forefinger. The easiest way to find it is to spread your hand wide, palm down, and then place the crease of the other thumb on the edge of the web. The tip of the thumb will be on the point, which is between the two bones. Pressure is exerted against the bone of the finger, not the thumb. It is usually quite sore. Massage firmly, first one hand and then the other, for three or four minutes on each hand.

Do not use this point if pregnant.

Other points to be massaged are the bladder meridian points, starting in the space between the bottom two ribs (BL 20) and moving down each side of the spine, all the way to the bottom of the tailbone. In addition, some people find it helpful to massage the centerline of the abdomen, moving down the center line with a snakelike (wiggling) motion. The abdomen can also be massaged, with a large circular motion.

When massaging the abdomen, it is important to respect the direction of the intestines. Looking at an anatomy book will give you a good picture. When using your hands in a circular motion on the abdomen, you always move them up the right side and down the left side. Facing the other person, the movement is always clockwise.

FATIGUE

Sometimes a person just feels tired or exhausted. This can be due to the normal stresses of life or to overwork. Restoring energy and a sense of vitality and well-being is important in this circumstance.

The primary approach to restoring energy and vitality is to attempt to balance the flow of the energy in the great central channel as well as to harmonize the various functions of the body through the yu points on the bladder meridian on the back.

Begin with the person lying on her or his back. After doing a general opening sequence as described in Chapter 8, proceed as follows:

193

- Do firm pressure massage to the point at the top of the head directly above the tips of the ears on the central line (GV 20, Bai Hui). Follow this with firm pressure massage of the points across the base of the skull, under the bone, pressing up into the bone.
- Now gently massage the area on the exterior of the front of the chest on either side, which is about three finger widths beneath the breastbone, in the hollow of the shoulder but against the rib cage. This point (LU 1) will be quite tender. By massaging the area carefully, you will stimulate the point as well as the general area, which has many lymph nodes and is therefore important to the immune system.

- Now, position yourself at the side of the person and place one hand on the upper center of the chest. With the hand, press in this order: CV 17, in the middle of the sternum, midpoint between the nipples; CV 12, on the centerline, midway between the navel and the diaphragm; and CV 6, about three finger widths below the navel. On each point, hold for about two minutes and direct your own breath into the area. Hold an image of the energy flow in the central channel of the person. In this way, the channel can be opened and strengthened.

- With the person still on his or her back, slide one hand under the base of the neck, with the fingers firmly pressing into the spine. With the other hand, hold first the point on the spine halfway down on an imaginary horizontal line that is halfway between the tip of the wing bone (scapula) and the bottom of the rib cage, then the point halfway down from a horizontal line between the bottom of the rib cage and the top of the hipbone. Hold these points two or three minutes each. As before, breathe energy through your hands into this point and hold an image in your awareness of the energy flow in the great central channel.

- Now, with the hand closest to the head, apply pressure with your curved fingers to the point just out from the spine, in from the center of the scapula (BL 13). With the other hand, hold the points, an area at a time, down one side of the spine all the way to the hipbone. Hold the points for a minute or two, then move your hand down. Do this on both sides.

- Finally, with one hand, grasp the back of the Achilles tendon between your thumb and fingers as close to the heel as possible, and with the other hand massage the point hoku (LI 4) on the web of the hand in the joint (up high) between the thumb and the finger, against the finger. Work on both sides.

Do not use this point (LI 4) on a pregnant woman.

Use an ending sequence to finish balancing the energy.

FACIAL WRINKLES

195

There has always been a strong tradition in China for women to use acupressure for facial beauty. The following treatment may be done on oneself. It must be done repeatedly, over time, to have a lasting effect.

With your fingertips and thumbs, press all of the points around the eye sockets. Massage the upper and lower areas around the eyes from the inside to the outside, and across the brow.

Locate the point ST 2, which is to the side of the nose and about a finger width below the edge of the bone at the bottom of the eye, and on a straight line directly below the pupil. It will be a little tender. Use this as a beginning point and repeatedly massage first the point and then across the face, toward the upper ear. Each time you slide your fingers across the side of the cheek, make it a little lower until finally you end up on the jawbone.

Now massage the entire area of the scalp from the hairline to the top of the head, above the ears to the centerline.

Next, massage the face to the sides of the corners of the mouth.

Finally, massage the neck as follows: raise the chin as high as possible and massage the neck from behind the ear, down to the front center of the neck, and from the jawbone down toward the shoulder.

In addition to massaging all of the above points, it is useful to exercise all of the facial muscles by making faces and squiggling all of the muscles of the face.

13

Acupressure
for First Aid

Acupressure can be very helpful in emergency situations. There are times when first aid must be carried out before any other help can be used. Certain points are known for their ability to provide this first aid.

This information is not intended to substitute for medical care. Once again, appropriate medical care should always be sought when a serious condition exists and medical care is available. But there are times when it is not immediately available, and then knowing some of the things that can be done with acupressure can be of help.

There are a few points on the meridians that are known to have an immediate and strong action on the body. They should be used judiciously and only if their use is the only available alternative.

Generally, these first aid or emergency points are needled by acupuncture. However, they can be stimulated with finger pressure, by pressing firmly with the fingernail, or with a small pointed, but not sharp, stick.

HEMORRHAGING

Point SP 1 is used to stop bleeding and can stop even severe uterine hemorrhaging. The point is also reportedly capable of helping to restore consciousness. However, it appears that this is loss of consciousness due to bleeding, not from other causes.

SP 1 is located on the inside of the corner of the nail of the big toe (toward the body), at the base of the nail.

CONVULSIONS

Point GV 26 is used to stop convulsions due to either accident or epilepsy. It is also used to aid in the restoration of consciousness in the case of fainting.

GV 26 is located immediately below the center of the nose, on the upper lip.

SHOCK

Point CV 1 is known to be very useful in extreme emergency situations where the person is unconscious from shock, trauma, or drowning. It is known as a revival point. It can be stimulated very firmly—many times, if the situation is desperate. In cases of severe drowning, the use of a needle inserted up to one inch has been effective.

CV 1 is located halfway between the anus and the genitals, on the perineum, in the exact center. On a man, the point is one-half inch from the edge of the tissue around the anus, on the center line.

DIFFICULT CHILDBIRTH

SP 6 is an emergency point for a variety of difficulties during and following labor: difficulty in delivery, in delivery due to excessive movement of the baby, and in difficulty delivering the afterbirth. Also, known to help when there is excessive bleeding after birth, when the patient loses consciousness, with severe uterine hemorrhaging, and when the baby dies in the uterus.

SP 6 is located on the inside of the leg, three finger widths above the anklebone, a quarter inch behind (to the rear of) the bone. The three yin meridians of the leg cross at this point.

Point GB 21 will stimulate labor if it is difficult. However, it must not be used if there is a history of any heart problems. This point is located on the top of the shoulder, halfway between the base of the neck and the end of the clavicle, on top of the muscle, where it will divide upon pressure.

Threatened Breech Birth

When a breech birth is threatened, point BL 67 is known to correct the baby's position in the uterus. It should be used far enough in advance to allow for the turning of the baby. Moxa may be used for this purpose if it's very close to time of deliver, as this point can induce labor. It is located on the lower outside corner of the small toenail.

14

Using Moxa
for Self Help

Moxa is widely used in the home in China and Japan for self treatment. It is used by people to treat themselves and their friends, and by parents to treat their children. It is considered an easy and effective way to treat minor ailments. It is often used in the colder areas of these countries because of its ability to dispel cold and damp, two contributors to many common complaints. Use of heat is very comforting when these cold climatic conditions are present.

Traditionally, moxabustion has been used as a part of acupuncture to treat the problems caused by disorders of deficiency of chi and those caused by these cold climatic conditions. Moxa is warming and drying. It is used in acupuncture either as its own treatment or as a way of stimulating (heating) the needles, in order to stimulate the points even more.

Moxa is the herb artemisia, in several varieties. Chinese moxa and European moxa are both widely used all over the world. It is easily cultivated. Generally, it is aromatic when burned, and some say it smells like marijuana. One should be aware that neighbors might comment if much of it is burned in the home.

Chinese moxa is obtainable in loose, bulk form, and in rolls, the outside of which is made of firm paper, making it appear to be a large cigar. There is also a "smokeless" moxa stick that looks like a hard black cigar. Most forms are available in Chinese herb stores or by mail order. (See Resources.)

The Japanese also use Akabane stick, which is a sticklike incense covered with a mixture of green herbs. It is used in the same way as a moxa roll.

The use of moxa as described here is very limited. It is presented for self-help purposes only. Anyone wishing to pursue the study of the use of moxa should take a course and buy a good book on the subject. Our focus is on the use of the moxa roll because of its ease of use and safety considerations. The moxa roll is the most convenient and the safest way of using moxa. The direct placement of burning moxa, common in acupuncture, is in fact quite risky except in the hands of a trained professional.

In general, moxa is burned so the heat stimulates either a single point or an entire area, including several points. The stimulation is very noticeable when the point becomes sufficiently hot. The heat used is considerable. However, it is always removed before there is a chance of burning the skin.

In using moxa rolls, you may find that where you were unsure of the exact location of a point—on the back of the arm,

202

for instance—it will become obvious when the moxa is used. The heat from the tip of the roll will warm the entire area, but the exact point will be decidedly felt as a tingle or even like a needle prick.

HOW TO USE MOXA

Moxa wool, or punk, can be used if you desire. There are other methods used by acupuncturists.

First, the skin is protected from overheating with a thin slice of fresh gingerroot placed on the skin over the point. (Sometimes a slice of fresh garlic is used.) The use of the ginger also adds its own heating properties to those of the moxa.

A small piece of the moxa wool is then formed into a cone about a half inch across and an inch high. (The moxa ball can range from pea size to the size of a large bean.) This little "tipi" of moxa is placed on the slice of ginger and then lit with a burning stick of incense (the easiest and safest way), so the heat stimulates the skin. This is repeated with more cones of moxa if further stimulation is needed. If the moxa becomes too hot, it can be knocked off onto a plate, or the entire slice of ginger can be lifted off the skin.

The tip of the roll is lit with a match and then blown upon until the entire end of the roll has become a glowing coal, like a cigar burning. Ash will form as it burns, and this ash must be periodically removed. Have a plate handy for this purpose and to safely place the burning roll when it's not being used.

When you have ended a moxa treatment, place the end of the roll in a bowl of sand to extinguish it, or use a very sharp

203

knife to cut off the burning end. In this way you can save the unburned portion of the roll for later use. Some people use the metal canister from a roll of film as a way of extinguishing the moxa roll.

The burning end of the roll can be used in two ways:

1. *Rotation.* The end of the roll is moved in a circular rotation over the area to be heated, keeping it far enough away from the skin so there is no danger of burn, but close enough to thoroughly warm the area. Repeated circling of the area can achieve a very warming effect as the heat is absorbed by the skin.

2. *Sparrow Pecking.* The tip is moved very close to the point and then pulled back before the skin is burned. The tip of the roll must not touch the skin, but it does come very close to the point. To prevent accidental movement from causing the tip of the moxa roll to touch the skin, rest the base of the hand on the body for steadiness. The method of sparrow pecking produces the maximum stimulation possible with the moxa roll.

Do not use moxabustion on anyone who has diabetes, is very old, is very young, or has varicose veins or any skin ailment. Diabetics often have lowered sensitivity to the heat and cannot feel it before burning occurs. Also, the skin of diabetics often has a greatly reduced capacity to heal. As for older people and small children, they have tender skin that burns easily.

MOXABUSTION TO
TREAT SPECIFIC AREAS

Any of the easily accessible points described in this book can be used with moxabustion, with the few exceptions we've noted, such as forbidden points during pregnancy. Some specific ways to use moxa that take advantage of its unique properties will be described.

Many people use moxa during the cold times of the year, when they feel affected by either cold or dampness. The feeling may be one of chilliness or shivering, or a sense that one may be getting a cough or cold because of the weather. Or, one may feel stiff or actually have some mild arthritic pains due to the damp and cold.

If a person feels heated, has hot arthritis, or senses a fever coming on (such as from influenza), moxa should not be used. A Chinese doctor may use moxa in a wide range of conditions, but moxa should not be used by an untrained person when heat is present.

Chest Area

Often, the first sense of cold will be in the chest area. The moxa can be used to warm the entire area of the chest using the rotation method. The upper chest is particularly amenable to this method. Most people find the warmth of the roll very comforting. This warming can be done for many minutes. Be certain to cover the chest following the use of the moxa and to keep warm.

Remember that the heat will tend to open the pores of the skin, making one more susceptible to invasion.

Hands and Feet

The hands and feet may become quite cold. The heat of the moxa can be used as a general source of heat. Using the rotation method, you may find that particular points or areas seem to feel better with the heat, and they can be further stimulated using the sparrow pecking method, if desired.

Specific Points

The CV 17 point is located on the chest on the central line, even with the nipples. It is very good for relieving chest congestion and coughs. It has also traditionally been used for asthma and excessive coughing of mucus. You can use the moxa roll to stimulate this point. Heat the point to where you must stop, let the point cool, and repeat. You can repeat up to five times.

The GB 35 point is located on the outside of the lower leg, halfway between the knee and the ankle. It is very good for relieving cold feet and also if the chest feels congested. It is traditionally used for a wide variety of ailments but is well-known for its ability to relieve even severe chest congestion. Use the pecking method until the point is very hot. Let it cool, then repeat three times.

Joints of the Fingers

These are points on the two sides of the last joint of any finger of the hand. These points can be used whenever there are the pains of cold arthritis in that particular finger. Be sure not to use the moxa if there is swelling and heat. Use the pecking motion of the roll to stimulate these points. You can repeat this two times if desired.

Points on the Back of the Wrists

The points on the back of the wrists (and the points in the couple of inches above them on the lower arm) are key points on the yang meridians of the arms. When a person is suffering from cold or a heat deficiency, stimulating the yang meridians can be very warming to the body. The best way to know is to try it on yourself.

207

CONCLUSION

The practice of acupressure can become a very important part of one's life. For some, it is so natural to use touch on another person to bring well-being and caring that study only furthers the practice. For others, entering the world of acupressure is a revelation that the wonderful world of disciplined human touch can bring enormous benefit and comfort to others. And, some also discover, it brings about a profound sense of accomplishment in a tangible way: we can experience the results.

By now, you've probably learned that I believe in bringing an inner discipline to personal practice. For me, it is the only real approach to acupressure. Others may stress learning more and more technique in order to achieve proficiency. However, nothing can replace the experience of chi in the body.

You will find out how you best experience the chi in another person. From the practice that you have done while learning from this book, take the time to reflect on what your experience has been as you worked on yourself and others.

Many feel chi in their hands and with their fingertips and know exactly what is going in the body of the person that they are touching. Some, as with many acupuncturists, can make a decision in their minds about what needs to be done. Others will feel or sense what needs to be done and their hands seem to carry it out with great precision.

Most people will discover that if they focus their awareness on their own inner flow of breath, of chi, of sensations in their hands and arms, and of the inner feelings and imagery that arise within as they are doing acupressure, that they will know what is going on.

This is not always easy to do.

When a feeling arises, or an image floats through one's consciousness or at the back of one's mind, just on the edge of consciousness, it's a challenge to understand its significance. The best advice that can be given is to trust in your instincts. If you suddenly feel sad, angry, or as if a dark cloud is descending upon your shoulders, and if this happens in the middle of an otherwise pleasant and relaxing session of acupressure on a sunny afternoon, trust your instincts that you have activated a difficult area in the person you are working on.

Trust that you can be helpful and that you can change whatever it is that you have found. The sensitivity that led you to this awareness is the same sensitivity that can help the process of change and healing. If it is a difficult emotional experience that has been activated in the other person, remember that it would

210

not have come up if it were not ready to be worked on. It came up because you are there.

The human organism sets its own pace for growth and change and healing. When you put yourself in the place of activating and working with the chi energy, trust that it will go its course, but in its own way and time.

Often, the person you work on will be relieved of pain or discomfort quite rapidly. But in other instances, whatever has been causing difficulty has been doing so for a while, and it will take time for the person's body to experience the changes of energy that have come about through the acupressure you have done. You will often be asked, "Am I better now," or, "Is the problem gone?" and similar questions, as if you had x-ray vision. You may have sensitive hands, but you cannot know the future for certain. Tell the person that all change takes time.

You will want to study other books on acupressure, including shiatsu, tui na, Touch for Health, Jin Shin Do, Jin Shin Jitsu, reflexology, craniosacral work, and so forth. No single book can even begin to cover the vast range of discoveries of the specific points that can be used, the ways to activate them, and the proper sequence in which to use them. This kind of detailed knowledge comes from a lifetime of work and study, and only becomes meaningful as the need for this knowledge arises as work on others.

Work on others and learn from your own practice and from what everyone else can teach you. Enjoy the journey

RESOURCES

ACUPRESSURE SUPPLIES
(Including Charts and Moxa Rolls)

Chinese Herbal Center
28 Bowery
New York, NY 10013
212-732-0923

Chong Wah Center
1032 South Jackson Street
Seattle, WA 98104
206-323-7229

**Comjam Chinese Herb
Company**
1768 Stockton Street
San Francisco, CA 94133
415-433-9851

**Greenlake Herbs & Chinese
Medicine Clinic**
1111 North 82nd Street
Seattle, WA 98103
206-525-5825

Hai Kang Co.
917 Harrison Street
Oakland, CA 94607
510-451-2422

Jen Tai Chinese Herbal Center
531 Southwest 3rd Avenue
Portland, OR 97204
503- 228-3235

Tai Fong Wo Herbs
857 Washington Street
San Francisco, CA 94108
415- 982-2195

INTERNET RESOURCES

Acupressure Institute of America (acupressure.org): This is the home page of the Acupressure Institute in Berkeley, California, Michael Reed Gach's school. It has an online resource center of books, charts, and other resources, as well as a description of the school and the courses.

Acupuncture Products Supply Inc. (acupuncture.hypermart.net): E-mail: acupuncturesupply@usa.net

Alternative Health Resource Center (flowofqi.com): Probably the best online resource center for information on the entire area of acupressure, body therapy, and massage. Lots of links to other sites and resources.

British Columbia Acupressure Association (islandnet.com/~bcata): This is their home page, with much useful information about acupressure, descriptions of courses and classes available, and links to other acupressure resources.

QI Journal (qi-journal.com): This is a very good online journal, and it has many interesting articles and features, including the interactive acuman—a model of a person you can rotate at will; locate all of the points on the meridians; and activate a point to get a full description of its location, name, and use in acupressure.

Sensory Awareness Foundation (sensoryawareness.org/schedule.html): A great introduction to sensory awareness. Also, a complete list of workshops, instructors, and practitioners.

Swedish Institute (schools.naturalhealers.com/swedish): This accredited New York school has a complete program of acupressure, and the home page has all of the information.

SCHOOLS

There are very few schools in North America that teach only acupressure. However, there are schools that teach shiatsu, and colleges and universities that teach TCM and acupuncture. These schools often offer courses for nondegree students in chi gung and t'ai chi.

Academy of Chinese Culture & Health Sciences

A training program for acupuncturists, this Chinese Cultural Center also offers classes in t'ai chi and chi gung taught by the Chinese master who directs the school. There is also a low cost clinic where acupressure is part of the offered treatments.

> 1601 Clay Street
> Oakland, CA 94612
> 510-763-7787

Acupressure Institute

Michael Reed Gach founded the first acupressure only training program in North America. Drawing on the resources of the Bay area, the school has an outstanding faculty and a bookstore. There is a Chinese herb store in conjunction with it. It includes an entire resource center for Traditional Chinese Medicine, with the exception of acupuncture.

> 1533 Shattuck Avenue
> Berkeley, CA 94709
> 510-845-1059 and 800-442-2232

Jin Shin Do Foundation for Bodymind Acupressure

This school was founded by Iona Marsaa Teeguarden, and practitioners are trained here in her unique style of acupressure, using her trademarked Jin Shin Do points. While based on TCM, Teeguarden has chosen to work with only points related to the strange flows. Certified training in massage therapy.

> 1084G San Miguel Canyon Road
> Royal Oaks, CA 95076
> 831-763-7702

Oregon College of Oriental Medicine

This certified acupuncture school offers several levels of training in traditional chi gung by a Chinese master. The courses are open to all.

> 10525 Southeast Cherry Blossom Drive
> Portland, OR 97216
> 503-253-3443

215

Sensory Awareness Foundation

This is the school founded by Charlotte Selver, who at the age of 100 still teaches workshops at such places as Green Gulch Ranch. The original work of Elsa Gindler in sensory awareness is taught by many practitioners. Workshops in sensory awareness are held throughout the United States and in other countries.

955 Vernal Avenue
Mill Valley, CA 94941

Swedish Institute, School of Massage Therapy, and School of Acupuncture

This long established professional school of Swedish style massage now is fully accredited in acupuncture and teaches Traditonal Chinese Medicine. The Body Therapy/Massage Training Program has two separate tracks, one of them TCM-based acupressure.

226 West 26th Street
New York, NY 10001
212- 924-5900

BIBLIOGRAPHY

ACUPRESSURE

Chinese Massage—A Handbook of Therapeutic Massage. Vancouver, B.C., Canada: Hartley & Marks, Ltd., 1987.

An excellent, clear, and well-illustrated guide to the use of traditional Chinese acupressure as practiced today in a medical setting. In fact, it was developed in the Anhui Medical School Hospital, Peoples Republic of China. Almost too many details on technique, and some of the clinical applications will not be of use. A fantastic book nevertheless.

Gach, Michael Reed, Ph.D. *Acupressure's Potent Points: A Guide to Self-Care for Common Ailments.* New York: Bantam Books, 1990.

———. *Arthritis Relief at Your Fingertips.* New York: Warner Books, 1989.

———. *The Bum Back Book.* Berkeley, CA: Ten Speed Press, 1996.

The founder and director of the Acupressure Institute has written several self-help books for the lay person. Gach is a great believer in the use of yoga positions as well as acupressure points for self-help. This is especially apparent in *The Bum Back Book*. Many, many people have been helped by his books. Well-illustrated and clearly written, though short on the basics of Chinese medicine. The book on arthritis relief is excellent, and *The Bum Back Book* has quite literally kept people out of surgery.

Li Hui, Jiu, and Jia Zhao Xiang (trans. Jiang Qi Yuan, M.D. and Gao Ying Mao). *Pointing Therapy—A Chinese Traditional Therapeutic Skill*. Beijing, Peoples Republic of China: Shandong Science and Technology Press, 1996.

This is an extremely interesting modern book on the use of Chinese acupressure for a wide range of serious medical conditions. The translation is not the best English, and the meridians and points are designated only by their Chinese names, making this book a lot of work to use. But the locations of the points are clearly given, and the techniques used are extensive and complete.

Serizawa, Katsusuke, M.D. *Tsubo—Vital Points for Oriental Therapy*. Tokyo: Japan Publications, Inc, 1998.

This book has been in print for years, and deservedly so. It is probably the best and clearest book in the English language on using shiatsu on the meridians and their points for medical (and some nonmedical) conditions. Complete treatment patterns are given, and the book is extremely well-illustrated.

Teeguarden, Iona Marsaa. *Acupressure Way of Health*, Jin Shin Do. New York: Harper & Row, 1978.

The founder of Jin Shin Do School of Acupressure details her selection of thirty acupressure points and the use of them. Teeguarden has strayed far from Traditional Chinese Medicine, even giving traditional points new numbers, which can be confusing and misleading. Some find her approach of using a few set treatment patterns perfect for their sensibilities. Others find it limited. Very well-illustrated and clear.

TRADITIONAL CHINESE MEDICINE

The Barefoot Doctor's Handbook, Geographic Health Studies, 1994.

A manual originally published in 1970 by the Institute of Traditional Chinese Medicine of Hunan Province to meet the working needs of rural doctors. This famous book became the handbook for the program of the Chinese government to bring health care to everyone in modern China. The book was so useful that the United States government translated and published an American edition for use in rural America. The manual is divided into seven chapters. It lists some 197 diseases, 522 herbs (with 338 illustrations), has a major section on first aid—including bone-setting and emergency procedures—and a clear section on meridians and points. The section on Chinese medicine includes acupuncture, acupressure, and moxabustion, and a comprehensive listing of acupuncture points and their usage.

Butt, Gary Chak-Kei, and Frena Bloomfield. *Harmony Rules—The Chinese Way of Health Through Food.* New York: Samuel Weiser, Inc., 1987.

Do not think this is a book just about food. Butt is a highly trained Chinese doctor in China who uses acupressure, herbs, and food, as well as acupuncture. Bloomfield is a former student. The two have written one of the clearest introductions to the basics of Chinese medicine in the English language. There is an enormous amount of concrete information that will be useful to the acupressurist. Basic conditions of yin and yang imbalances are described in an understandable way. Diagrams of the meridians from the Ming Dynasty are fascinating.

Hoizey, Dominique and Marie-Joseph. *A History of Chinese Medicine.* Scotland: Edinburgh University Press, 1993 (out-of-print but available).

A delightfully written and enjoyable history written for the general reader as well as the serious student. Beautiful illustrations and lots of quotations from traditional sources.

219

Bibliography

Jianping, Huang. *Methodology of Traditional Chinese Medicine.* Beijing, Peoples Republic of China: New World Press, 1995.

An exceedingly well-written, clear, and scholarly book on the theory of Chinese medicine. The history of the development of Chinese medicine is given in the context of both Eastern and Western philosophy, and the quotations from the oldest sources are most interesting. An outstanding contribution to the science of medicine.

Kaptchuk, Ted J., OMD. *The Web That Has No Weaver—Understanding Chinese Medicine.* Lincolnwood, Illinois: Contemporary Books, 1999.

Perennially a favorite in the United States, this book is complete as to theory and detail. Many will find it difficult to read, but if the information on theory is required, it is here. People who love the intricacies of Chinese diagnostic language will love this book.

Mann, Felix, LMCC. *The Meridians of Acupuncture.* London: William Heinemann Medical Books, Ltd, 1999.

One of many books by the great contemporary British acupuncturist, this one is excellent for its clear descriptions of the meridians. Extensive charts show all the meridians, not just the main ones. Dr. Mann also gives us traditional descriptions of the functions of the main meridians not often found in other books. An outstanding book and useful to the acupressurist.

Shen, Nong. *Canon of Herbs.*

Not readily available except in libraries, this book was written in the first and second centuries and is the earliest extant book on Chinese pharmacology. It summarizes the experience of the ancient Chinese in using medicinal substances.

Tin Yao So, Dr. James. *The Book of Acupuncture Points.* Brookline, Massachusetts: Paradigm Publications, 1985.

This is an outstanding book on the traditional uses of the meridian points. It is clear and has good illustrations. It cross-indexes points by location, use, symptoms, name, and number. Its weakness is that it does not tell you how to use the points in a treatment pattern.

The Yellow Emperor's Canon of Medicine.

Some ancient books on Traditional Chinese Medicine and pharmacology have played an important role in developing the science of modern Chinese medicine. This book is probably the most important. Written by unknown medical scholars during the Warring States Period (475-221 BC), this was the first complete summary of ancient Chinese medicine. It explains human anatomy, physiology, pulse, diagnosis, and treatment.

Zhongjing, Zhang. *Treatise on Febrile Diseases Caused by Cold* and *Synopsis of Prescriptions of the Golden Chamber.*

These two books are considered by some to be the most important classics of Traditional Chinese Medicine, written some 1,700 years ago by Zhang Zhongjing, the great sage of Traditional Chinese Medicine. They are still used by students as textbooks in all colleges of TCM, and as reference books by medical practitioners and scholars in the field.

INDEX

B

227

229

Neck stretch, 124
Newborn infants, 147

O

Oil, massage, 135
Olfactory information, 128
Organ meridians related to
    pulses, 130, 131
Organs, yin and yang, 18

P

Palms of the hands, 118
Pathogens, 26
Patting, 122
Perception, inner, 141
Pericardium 6, 155
Pericardium meridian, 72–73
Physical exercise, 26, 29–30
Points, five controlling
    Bladder 54: entrusting middle,
        151, 155, 173, 174, 180
    Large Intestine 4, 155
    Lung 7, 154–55
    Pericardium 6, 155
    Stomach 36, 154
Points, holding, 125–26
Points, key
    Bladder 38, 150–51
    Bladder 54: entrusting
        middle, 151, 173, 174, 180
    Bladder 62, 152
    defined, 143
    five controlling points,
        154–55
    Gall Bladder 20, 150, 175
    Gall Bladder 21: shoulder
        well, 149, 175, 188
    Gall Bladder 31, 152–53

GV 20: bai hui, 61, 97,
    146–47, 191
Large Intestine 4: ho ku,
    153–54
on main organ meridians,
    144
shorthand names for, 145
SP 16: abdomen sorrow,
    148–49
Spleen 4, 71, 153
ST 16: chest window, 148
yu points, 95–96, 155–57
Pregnancy
    as cause for concern, 132
    forbidden points during, 185,
        188, 192, 195
    moxabustion and, 205
    precautions during, 164
Prenatal chi, 13, 14
Pressure
    acupressure and, 116
    advantages of using, 117
    elbow, 120–21
    fingertip exercise, 119–20
    palms of the hands, 118
    thumbs, 117–18
    tips of the fingers, 118–19
    using fingers together, 119
Protective chi, 13
Pruden, Bonnie, 33
Pulses, taking the, 128, 129–31

Q

Qi energy. *See* Chi
QI Journal, 214

R

Reflexology, 33, 115

231

232